RESUME SHORTCUTS

Career books by Robbie Miller Kaplan

101 Resumes For Sure-Hire Results

Resume Shortcuts

Resumes: The Write Stuff

Sure-Hire Cover Letters

Sure-Hire Resumes

The Whole Career Sourcebook

RESUME SHORTCUTS

How to Quickly Communicate Your Qualifications
With Powerful Words and Phrases

Robbie Miller Kaplan

IMPACT PUBLICATIONS
Manassas Park, VA

RESUME SHORTCUTS
How to Quickly Communicate Your Qualifications
With Powerful Words and Phrases

Library of Congress Cataloguing-in-Publication Data

Kaplan, Robbie Miller
     Resume shortcuts: how to quickly communicate your qualifications with powerful words and phrases / Robbie Miller Kaplan
          p. cm.
     ISBN 1-57023-071-4 (alk. Paper)
     1. Rèsumès (Employment) I. Title.
HR5383.K367 1997
808'.06665—dc21   96-53562
                                                         CIP

For information on distribution or quantity discount rates, Tel. 703/361-7300, Fax 703/335-9486, or write to: Sales Department, IMPACT PUBLICATIONS, 9104-N Manassas Drive, Manassas Park, VA 20111-2366. Distributed to the trade by National Book Network, 4720 Boston Way, Suite A, Lanham, MD 20706, Tel. 301/459-8696 or 800/462-6420.

Lovingly Dedicated
to My Support System
My Husband Jim and My Daughters Julie and Samantha

Acknowledgments

I could not have completed this book without the inspiration and support of my clients.

A special thank you to my good friend Wade Robinson, and to Nancy Sullivan, Betty McManus, Mary Fairchild, Jeff Held, and the Fairfax County Government Personnel Department and Commission for Women.

A big thank you to my mother, Jean Miller, a retired English teacher who not only fostered my love for reading and writing but did the first edit of the manuscript.

Contents

Introduction

It's tough to write resumes. While articulating your strengths, experiences, accomplishments, and contributions on paper is difficult, it can be downright overwhelming if it has to be done at the last minute.

New resume terminology only adds to the confusion. Maybe you've heard about electronic resumes and scanning systems and now you're wondering if you'll need to write not just one, but maybe three resumes. You're also faced with the option of mailing or faxing your resume—which delivery system will be best?

I have been helping job seekers write resumes for 14 years and I am still baffled that individuals who can direct staffs of 125, develop and manage multi-million dollar budgets, write award-winning proposals, research and defend doctoral dissertations, or consistently achieve 130 percent of sales goals can write such boring, bland, and unappealing resumes that reflect experience and skills well below their capabilities.

If you're paralyzed by the resume writing process, procrastinated so long you've run out of time, or facing a blank page and need a resume fast, *Resume Shortcuts* will simplify the process, help you sort through the options, and enable you to produce a professional and "sure-hire" resume, efficiently and effectively.

Resume Shortcuts is filled with tips on writing summaries, experience descriptions, education, skills, and the latest how to's on traditional, electronic, and scannable resumes.

Resume Shortcuts begins with the basics of resume writing. Hundreds of examples of well written, attention-grabbing sentences and paragraphs follow, organized by chapters for opening summaries and experience sections and cleverly worded entries for education, skills, awards, honors, certifications, professional affiliations, and publications that bolster your credentials while downplaying weaknesses. You can quickly locate suggestions, wording, sentences, and paragraphs for each section—personalize the information with your own data—assemble, and voilá—a resume. It sounds easy and it is!

Need some more inspiration? Check out the chapter on job-getting resume samples. You'll visualize how to pull it all together with 18 resumes from diverse occupations, chronological as well as functional examples, with effective ways to showcase strengths and minimize weaknesses. You'll see how to convert a traditional resume into a scannable one—then convert it again into an electronic one.

Still have some questions? Take a look at "Answers Please." I surveyed job seekers just like you and asked them what resume problems and questions puzzled them the most. I've included answers and suggestions for 34 of the toughest and most frequently asked questions.

Resume Shortcuts is a painless and sure-cure for resume paralysis. Use it to dazzle employers with imaginative, well-crafted wording and make your job search a success.

Good luck!

1

Basic Training

Technology has had a significant impact on how you present your qualifications, identify job leads, research and meet prospective employers, and distribute your credentials. While technology will continue to revolutionize the way you look for jobs, it will not replace the resume as a primary job-hunting tool. Resumes are still the first step in the job search process. Effective resumes market your skills, qualifications, and credentials to employers, arousing their interest and desire to meet you. Employers use resumes to screen and locate job candidates whose experience, education, training, and skills best meet their job requirements. A resume won't get you a job but a good one will initiate an invitation for an interview, an opportunity to sell yourself in person.

The best resumes reflect your strengths, skills, and accomplishments. They focus on what you've contributed and what you can offer an employer. Resumes that are most successful are targeted for the jobs you seek, demonstrating how your qualifications meet employer requirements.

If you are to compete effectively in your job search, you will have to write and produce resumes that keep pace with the dynamic changes in the workplace. Successful job seekers will research industries and organizations carefully to locate the best job opportunities and application requirements.

Terms and References You Need to Know About

- **ASCII (American Standard Code for Information Interchange):** Unformatted text, interchangeable and recognized by all word processing programs.

- **Computer-Based Applicant Tracking Systems:** Computer systems that scan resumes and identify job candidates that most consistently match specified employer job requirements.

- **Electronic Resume:** An unformatted resume prepared with ASCII text and sent via electronic mail.

- **E-Mail (Electronic Mail):** Mail sent or received electronically from one computer system to another computer system through a network.

- **Homepage:** The opening page of a set of hypermedia documents on the World Wide Web.

- **Hypermedia Document**: Series of pages created for Internet use combining text, graphics, and sound that link to other documents.

- **Internet:** A network of global computer networks enabling the access of information from all over the world.

- **Scannable Resume:** A paper or electronic resume created to match specific job requirements that will be read by "computer eyes," scanned by an automated resume processing system.

- **Traditional Resume:** A paper resume that will be read by "human eyes," quickly scanned to determine whether or not you meet job requirements.

- **World Wide Web (WWW):** A graphical system on the Internet that provides the ability to link documents across computer systems.

A significant development over the past decade is the use of computer-based applicant tracking systems—computerized systems that scan resumes. You'll find books and career experts that advise you to prepare separate resumes strictly for scanning purposes.

Before you spend a great deal of time and effort writing and producing totally different resumes, let's identify what types of organizations are acquiring these systems and the occupational areas they are recruiting.

A search on the Internet revealed that the largest companies along with county and state governments are the biggest users of resume scanning systems. Many of these organizations are the same ones that have downsized and laid off tens of thousands of workers in the last decade. An area hard hit during the days of "right sizing" was the human resource function. It seems these organizations have cut costs by replacing human resources with computer-based applicant tracking systems.

What types of employees are these large companies seeking? The greatest opportunities are for technical personnel with specific system experience in the programming, sales, design, application, analysis, support, program management, repair, and technical writing areas. You'll find few opportunities for management, administrative, and financial staff positions.

The scanning systems help employers screen resumes where the job applicants significantly exceed the job openings. For example, you'll find more and more school systems acquiring computer-based applicant tracking systems to screen teacher applicants.

Research tells us that employment opportunities have shifted from larger to smaller organizations. Half of all employed Americans currently work in organizations with fewer than 100 employees. More opportunities and new jobs will continue to grow with small companies. If the biggest companies are doing the least hiring and are continuing to downsize, it doesn't make sense to spend a lot of time preparing separate resumes for fewer job opportunities.

Computer-based applicant tracking systems are a reality and you'll find more companies using them as their prices decline. Maximize your efforts by researching companies of interest to learn their application preferences. You'll find web sites on the Internet providing explicit application procedures and organizational guidelines for scannable resumes.

The newspaper employment classified section details application processes too; recent advertisements required the majority of resumes to be mailed or faxed, but many technology-oriented companies requested resumes that could be scanned and requested or offered the option to forward via e-mail. One employer clearly stated: "All resumes are electronically scanned, processed, and distributed," while another detailed "A letter quality resume with a standard typeface is required (no underline or bold please)." If you're still in doubt, phone the company's human resource department to determine if they use computer-based applicant tracking systems and whether they have written application instructions.

Resume writing is a lot like child rearing. If you're looking for direction and guidance, you're likely to find contradictory theories and suggestions. What's foolproof advice? Follow all application directions as closely as possible. Some organizations will allow you up to seven pages for a scannable resume while others will tell you no more than two. If they want you to go back indefinitely with your work history, do so; but, if they want no more than ten years, give them just that. If an organization requests a social security number (most likely to do a security check), provide them your social security number if you want the job.

You can easily handle all these changes and adaptations by keeping a file of your resume in a computer. When you determine that a scanning system will be used, remove all special effects, as detailed in Chapter 8. As you read the job description or application requirements, tailor the resume to meet them. Save the file as a new document and you're ready to modify your resume for the next opportunity.

Traditional, Electronic, and Scannable Resumes

Resumes have been traditionally written to arouse an employer's interest in one's credentials and final copy printed on one to two pages of paper. These paper (**traditional**) resumes were and still are mailed and faxed to employers as well as hand-delivered by job candidates during networking, job fairs, and job interviews. **Traditional** resumes, still very much in use, are neither an endangered species or slated for extinction!

Electronic resumes differ significantly as they are written and transmitted via electronic medium, never paper. The **electronic** resume is prepared in a simple format as an ASCII file using a fixed-width font. The content can be identical to the **traditional** or the **scannable** resume.

Both **traditional** (paper) and **electronic** resumes are scanned by organizations using computer-based applicant tracking systems or resume scanning systems.

Scannable resumes are written and prepared for processing by a resume scanning system. While a **traditional** resume should captivate the human eye, **scannable** resumes have unique characteristics to attract the computer eye.

You will need a traditional resume, but you'll adapt and add to the information to create resumes for scanning and electronic mail purposes.

General Guidelines

Your resume, regardless of what type you choose to prepare, must be written and tailored to showcase your unique qualities and talents. While traditional, electronic, and scannable resumes all have distinct features which will be discussed in later chapters, there are basic guidelines for resume writing.

Chronological Versus Functional

There are two basic resume types, the chronological and functional. The following descriptions will help you choose the resume type that will better meet your needs.

The chronological resume is the most conventional, listing experiences and education in date order, beginning with the most recent and working backwards. It works best for individuals who have followed a career path with positions of increased responsibility. Some employers, particularly those in traditional industries or fields such as banking, accounting, or law, will only consider chronological resumes.

Because chronological resumes are structured in date order, they highlight gaps in employment, frequent or excessive job changes, and shifts in careers.

The functional resume organizes your work history by areas of expertise and experience such as managing, writing, training, or marketing. A work history, including job titles, places of employment, cities, states, and dates, is optional. I recommend that you include the work history because if it is omitted, employers will suspect you are hiding something and it may knock you out of the running.

The functional resume downplays gaps in employment and numerous job moves. It works best and is used most frequently by individuals who have been out of the workforce for some time or changing careers, transferring skills and experiences from one career to another.

Some employers are biased against the functional resume because they want to know where you worked and in what positions you acquired the experience and knowledge. If you are going to use the functional format, make the experience area as descriptive and specific as possible. Or, organize your experience in chronological order but use functional categories within the structure to showcase transferrable skills and experiences (see resume example on page 129).

Examples of chronological and functional resumes are in Chapter 10.

Organization

Create a format and organize your resume to emphasize your skills, abilities, and contributions. Think of your resume as a building with the foundation reversed; begin at the top with your strengths and follow with credentials of next importance.

Introduce yourself and your resume with a statement or summary that illustrates your background, credentials, and proficiencies.

Include a career objective if your job search is very focused and you can specifically state what type of position you are seeking and in what type of organization or industry. Employers are not interested in self-serving objectives that state what you want, where you hope to be, and not what you have to offer.

Begin with a summary or a career objective or, you may choose to use both. Be aware that many individuals have lots of experience and talents that qualify them for a cluster of jobs. A career objective that is too specific may knock you out of the running for other opportunities. Summaries can state all these talents without being too specific. You choose!

Follow with what's most valuable or impressive. Your education, experience, skills, or licenses? Include and add categories in order of employer desirability.

10 Tips for Writing Effective Resumes

1. Your resume must be clear and concise. Select verbs in the active voice; you'll minimize words and your text will be easier to read, more authoritative, forceful, and direct.

2. Misspelled words and grammatical errors are unacceptable. Use a dictionary and grammar book to check for errors. Avoid jargon.

3. If using an acronym, spell the word(s) or name out and follow with the acronym in parenthesis. Once stated in this form, you can use the acronym.

4. The tenses should all agree. Describe your present experience in the present tense and your past experience in the past tense. If you want to list experiences you are no longer handling in a current job, include these past experiences in a separate paragraph.

5. Edit your resume many times to make it as effective as possible. Use a synonym dictionary, thesaurus, and standard dictionary to locate synonyms and improve word choice.

6. Spell out numbers from 1 to 10 and use figures for numbers 11 plus. Always use figures when following a $. When mixing numbers in a paragraph, use all figures.

7. Balance all text with white space. Allow one-inch margins on the top, bottom, and sides of the page.

8. Traditional resumes should be one to two pages in length. If you have extensive experience and qualifications, it is fine to use two pages. If you have numerous publications, you may need to use three pages or more.

9. When using two pages, never use a two-sided copier and always put your name and page number on the succeeding pages.

10. Avoid staples and paper clip the pages together.

2

Powerful Summaries

Summaries are like appetizers, stimulating employer interest in your qualifications, whetting their appetite to learn more about you. Use summaries to begin your resume and showcase your strengths. Select information that reflects your experience, skills, expertise, versatility, and successes.

Employers want to know that you meet job requirements. The summary is a perfect place to demonstrate how your background meets the requirements of the jobs you seek.

The best summaries reveal what's special about you. Your first and opening sentence should state who you are and what kind of experience you offer. Are you a sales pro, educator, special education teacher, financial professional, attorney, business attorney, marketing executive, or senior executive? Add some adjectives to your occupation and background and create a dynamite introduction.

Summary Opening Sentence Examples

- Experienced attorney with acknowledged expertise in immigration and nationality law.

- Data processing professional with over 16 years of progressive life cycle experience.

- Dynamic interior designer, successfully translating client needs and delivering diverse projects from inception to completion.

- Mathematician and computer scientist specializing in the fields of software development, computer programming, combinatorics, data and algorithm analysis, number theory, and graph memory.

- Senior executive with management background in sales and marketing, finance, and operations with organizational responsibility of up to 140 people.

- Experienced psychiatrist with a specialty in psychotherapy, family systems theory, family relationships issues, and medication management.

- Over ten years of progressive experience in all phases of electrical contracting working with commercial, industrial, and residential projects.

- Marketing professional with more than 15 years of progressive experience in domestic and international hotel marketing, sales, and operations.

- Experienced association director with strong background in membership services, convention planning, and customer services.

- Education professional with extensive experience in suburban and inner city schools.

- Solid background in managing corporate real estate projects and portfolios.

- Skilled trainer and manager with extensive experience developing and conducting training programs.

- Dedicated sales professional with consistent top sales performance.

- Food service professional with 15 years of rapid, progressive growth and advancement.

The opening sentence may suffice or you might want to add some spice. Determine your strongest skills and proficiencies. Select areas of expertise and specialties. Are you successful, a consistent performer, or skilled? Are you a recognized expert or specialist? What work characteristics set you apart from the pack?

Summary Examples

- Skilled professional with a proven record managing multiple real estate development projects and large budgets with optimal results. Effective leader, training and motivating staff to achieve dynamic performance.

- Enthusiastic and energetic sales professional with superior performance and exceptional interpersonal skills. Natural sales ability and expertise in building relationships and promoting long-term client loyalty by identifying and satisfying specific needs while exceeding expectations.

- Retail professional with 11 years of rapid, progressive growth and advancement. Solid record in identifying strategic growth opportunities and increasing profitability levels.

- Extensive and progressive experience in trust banking. Self-starter with expertise in estate settlement, complex trust issues, and investment management.

- Evidence technician with 30 years experience in large urban and small town police departments. Specialize in handling major incidents and crime scenes including homicide, death, bombings, and fires.

- Biologist with an expertise in insects, freshwater ecology, horticulture, and integrated pest management. Skilled in translating technical information into readily understandable language, appropriate for specific audiences.

- Resourceful and innovative retail professional with 12 years of experience establishing and operating retail stores. Proactively respond to strategic challenges driven by customer and business requirements.

- Accomplished manager with over ten years experience in hotel marketing, sales, and operations. Demonstrated success securing multiple targets including leisure, corporate, association, government, and tour groups. Expertise in advertising, pricing, development, and packaging.

- Senior executive with a proven record in restructuring operations and significantly improving bottom line performance. Visionary, skillfully increasing business volumes and penetrating markets.

- Skilled Systems Analyst with versatile technical ability applicable to all technologies. Team player, consistently demonstrating a sense of ownership for the success of team efforts. Computer expertise including hardware, software, and system planning, installation, administration, user training, troubleshooting, data recovery, and repair. Proficiently identify and utilize technology to improve, simplify, and expedite work and organizational priorities.

- Over 20 years experience as a volume jewelry buyer with large-scale retail and wholesale operations. Expertise in purchasing rough and polished diamonds to meet customer needs at the lowest wholesale cost.

- Senior executive with management background in sales, marketing, finance, and operations with organizational responsibility of up to 150 employees. Specialize in generating new business and developing strong trusting relationships with clients at all organizational levels.

- Sales pro with top performance in the telecommunications industry. Enthusiastic team player with a persistent approach to identifying and closing sales.

- Enthusiastic, focused, and innovative sales professional with a proven record of developing client relationships and providing legendary service.

- Top sales manager with solid experience successfully building and managing sales operations and developing sales staff and markets to consistently exceed organizational goals.

- Manager and trainer with broad and extensive experience in health care. Proactive team player, aggressively implementing company's strategies.

- Strong background in administrative operations, sales, and marketing developed from establishing and managing a video rental business.

- Successful business owner and manager with a proven record of creating and building a profitable events and meeting planning business.

- Skilled food service manager with excellent culinary skills. Extensive experience in fine dining restaurants, luxury hotels, conference centers, and institutional operations.

- Hotel professional with over 20 years of experience managing housekeeping and laundry functions. Exceptional leader who meets and thrives on the challenges of managing a diverse workforce. Fluent in Spanish, French, and English.

- Internationally acclimated individual. Extensive and rewarding international experiences, living and working in diverse countries, easily assimilating different cultures by adapting and communicating effectively.

- Qualified and innovative senior executive with progressive experience in all phases of association management. Careful and thorough planner, executing projects with discipline and undiverted attention to detail.

- Human resources manager with experience in compensation design, benefits administration, executive recruitment, training, and employee development in the retail industry.

- Energetic executive with solid achievements in strip mall development. Resourceful and innovative leader willing to take risks while meeting and exceeding aggressive financial goals.

- Seasoned financial manager, adept at analyzing complex business issues and producing "common sense" solutions. Diverse background with Federal, state, and local governments. CPA and CIA.

- Skilled, organized, and stable restaurant manager with over 11 years of experience planning, opening, and managing restaurants into successful operations.

- Hospitality and meeting planning professional with over eight years experience in national and on-property hotel sales. Consistent sales achiever with excellent communication and interpersonal skills.

- Dedicated leader with broad experience and commitment to secondary student athletes and athletic programs. Adept at fostering professionalism and communication with coaches and athletic administrators, demanding the highest levels of integrity while emphasizing the safety and well being of student athletes through a progressive sports medicine and coaching education program.

- Ten years experience as a librarian in academic and public settings. Expertise in applying and utilizing computer technology and Internet access to meet user needs.

- Marketing professional with a proven record of promoting concepts and products that consistently increase sales and capture new markets.

- Quality-oriented manager, successfully motivating and leading staffs while sustaining morale and meeting tight deadlines during major downsizings and reorganizations.

- Solid sales professional with exceptional people skills. Diplomatic problem-solver handling all personalities with finesse.

- Systems analyst with extensive experience managing and administering Local Area Networks (LANs) and Wide Area Networks

(WANs). Exceptional communicator, easily explaining all aspects of system operations to both technical and lay personnel.

- Experienced office manager, calmly and capably bringing a sense of order and organization to each office responsibility. Solid background in dental and medical office operations.

- Skilled facilitator and organizational development practitioner, stimulating organizations to explore, identify, and implement creative approaches to policies and practices that improve productivity and enhance performance.

- Marketing and sales professional with ten years of experience promoting concepts and products that consistently build sales and revenue. Expertise in conceptualizing strategies that capture new markets and increase client profitability.

- Librarian with diverse experience in academic and public settings. Specialist in applying and utilizing computer technology to meet user needs.

- Competent and responsible Registered Nurse with a solid background in trauma and emergency care. Extensive experience in metropolitan and suburban hospital settings. Fluent in spoken and written Spanish and English.

10 Tips for Creating Powerful Summaries

1. Prepare the employer for what's to come by titling the summary section appropriately. Choose from diverse headings including Career Summary, Background Summary, Qualifications Summary, Career Highlights, Career History, Professional Profile, Profile, Career Profile, or Summary of Experience.

2. Headings that fit best for a recent college graduate are Background Summary or Qualifications Summary.

3. A career professional may choose Professional Profile for their heading while a career changer might select Career Highlights or Summary of Experience.

4. Summaries can be as short as one or two sentences or as expansive as two to four bullets.

5. Decide what your best and strongest qualifications, strengths, and accomplishments are and how you want to feature and set these apart.

6. Use graphics in traditional resumes to draw the reader's eye to the summary. Try a ruling line either above the heading or both above the heading and below the last sentence.

7. Select appropriate and accurate adjectives that best describe your qualifications and traits. Try unique, exceptional, excellent, strong, qualified, skilled, productive, or successful.

8. If you have a credential that is so desirable, you can include it in the summary as well as the appropriate section (for example, security clearances).

9. Employers are most interested in hard facts. They're turned off by summaries that are light on experience but overloaded with self management skills and personality traits.

10. Make sure that your experience fully supports the information in your summary.

3

Experience Grabbers

While all sections that follow summaries support your opening statements, the experience section of your resume is actually the heart—it shows where you developed the skills and expertise and obtained the actual experience and accomplishments.

The best experience sections describe the scope and depth of your work experience while demonstrating your contributions and achievements.

Resumes are flat pieces of paper and you can make yours come alive by using descriptive opening statements for each work experience that illustrate the breadth, range, and size of your responsibilities, organization, product(s), and industry. Balance your content with action verbs that show strength and authority while detailing and quantifying wherever possible with nouns and adjectives.

Opening Statement Examples

- Direct an $8.4 million sales operation marketing international mailing services to corporate and government accounts in Northern California.

- Provided acute care nursing in a 10-bed CCU, caring for patients with a wide variety of cardiac problems from angina to cardiogenic shock.

- Established small business lending department within a commercial lending division of a local community bank. Successfully grew loan portfolio and other banking services resulting in bank assets in excess of $28 million.

- Create complex technical specifications for changes/modifications to an on-line ordering system including client-server GUI-based applications running on Unix-based workstations, PCs, and terminals.

- Manage food service operation and staff of 22 for a 245-room luxury property with combined banquet facilities for 700, 24-hour room service, fine dining restaurant, lounge, and employee cafeteria. Supervised stewarding department with a staff of 14.

- Market financial, leasing, and indirect loan services to automobile dealerships in the Commonwealth of Virginia.

- Plan, organize, direct, and control finance and accounting activities for an electronics components manufacturer with over $10.3 million in annual revenue.

Experience Statement Examples By Occupations

Accounting

- Perform all accounting functions for a major soil and environmental testing firm with three subsidiaries. Clients include all the major builders and developers in the local area.

- Handled accounting services for corporations in the real estate, communication, restaurant, transportation, and retail industries. Prepared monthly general ledgers, bank reconciliations, financial statements, trial balances, monthly payroll and sales taxes, quarterly reports, and corporate, federal, and state income taxes. Processed payroll and payroll summary reports.

- Establish and maintain depreciation schedules for a large financial institution on a computerized system. Prepare a monthly depreciation expense report.

- Executed all corporate accounting functions for a construction company. Analyzed fiscal month expense ledger for cost center managers and relocation, travel, and living expenses to monthly accruals.

- Prepared and controlled a complete set of books through trial balance. Handled the accounts payable and accounts receivable; coordinated the payroll for computerized processing.

- Prepared tax projections and tax returns for individuals, corporations, and partnerships.

- Analyzed cash flow and recommended effective programs to manage day-to-day operations of small businesses.

- Reviewed tax implications of retirement plans and recommended strategies to meet client needs.

- Oversaw all restaurant accounting functions including cost control, accounts payable, accounts receivable, general ledger, bank reconciliations, audits, monthly financial statements, and cash flow analysis.

- Assumed leadership of an accounting department that failed to accurately report financial statements. Established controls and quickly brought reporting requirements in compliance with accounting standards.

- Filed monthly, quarterly, and annual payroll, sales, and fuel tax returns.

- Write and present management letters that identify and propose cost-saving solutions that maximize efficiency.

Administrative Support

- Efficiently and effectively manage all administration and the myriad of details for a Fortune 100 senior executive.

- Assisted the top human resources executive for the corporation's largest operating division, employing approximately 58,000 personnel at 188 company-operated and franchised units in most states and countries.

- Answered multi-line phone system; screened and directed calls. Greeted and escorted clients to appointed locations.

- Maintained and controlled appointment calendar for senior executive, ensuring flexibility and availability. Circulated candidate and employment information throughout the division.

- Provide administrative support to five attorneys and three paralegals. Arrange meetings, maintain an up-to-date calendar; screen and refer telephone calls, answering inquiries where possible.

- Handled all administrative responsibilities for a large sporting goods retailer with three stores. Prepared, administered, and maintained payroll systems and benefits program. Processed expense reports; monitored approval and payment status.

- Answered phones and scheduled appointments for busy plumbing contractor. Produced client billings, ordered parts, and maintained accounts payable and filing system.

- Supported director and 3 managers of a 1,000-member professional association. Organized annual conference and meetings; created and maintained filing systems.

- Perform administrative support for a variety of firms through temporary placement assignments.

- Complete short- and long-term temporary assignments providing clerical support. Successfully handled clerical assignments at IBM

Corporation, First Union, and Marriott International.

- Prioritized and delegated daily work for five departmental administrative positions.

- Conceptualized and implemented an indexed records maintenance system for a newly-created department.

- Completed estimates and placed orders for a large glass company. Updated computerized inventory system. Compiled new employee packets and assisted with payroll. Maintained files and performed additional administrative duties as needed.

Auditing

- Work independently and as part of audit team performing operational, compliance, program, and financial audits for state government. Conduct each phase of audit process. Develop audit programs, participate in exit conferences, and write audit reports utilizing Lotus 1-2-3, WordPerfect, and EasyFlow.

- Acquired audit expertise performing financial compliance audits. Reconciled bank and financial records, conducted audit testing, documented results, and developed audit opinions.

- Primary client contact and supervisor on audit, review, and tax engagements for clients with $1 million to $60 million in gross revenue.

- Performed and supervised annual audits for financial institutions and organizations in insurance and employee benefit plan industries. Evaluated internal controls to comply with regulated industry requirements.

- Completed audits for profit-sharing, employee stock ownership, and self-funded health plans. Reviewed compliance with Department of Labor requirements and ERISA.

- Conducted certified audits of automobile dealerships and real estate management companies. Developed audit findings; wrote and edited audit reports.

Banking

- Promote bank services and sell checking and savings accounts, certificates of deposit (CDs), safe deposit boxes, and credit products. Utilize a thorough product knowledge to attract new business.

- Managed 170 estate, trust, agency, charitable, and escrow relationships for clients with investments ranging to $50 million.

- Performed internal audit of bank checks, certificates of deposit, safe deposit boxes, tellers cash, and cash items. Supervised staffs of eight to ten. Trained tellers on bank operations.

- Conducted research for consumer and commercial credit applications. Acquired information and performed credit analysis to determine whether to establish a relationship. Reviewed and evaluated assigned loans in the bank's personal loan program.

- Controlled and documented all credit union notes and loan applications. Audited notes and processed paid notes. Answered telephone inquiries from credit union members, car dealers, and insurance agents regarding accounts and loans.

- Handled teller operations for a busy suburban branch. Oversaw a daily cash drawer totaling over $120,000.

- Manage branch office of commercial national bank with $32 million in deposits. Oversee expenses and income, ensuring branch meets budget guidelines.

- Established the Mid-West Human Resources Division for one of the largest, independently-owned mortgage banking organizations. Met a two-week deadline in developing and implementing all human resources functions. Created and administered a benefit and compensation package.

- Increase commercial bank branch sales by prospecting new accounts and generating new business with existing accounts. Evaluate loan applications; recommend approval or decline.

- Selected to manage branch office during major bank merger. Oversaw conversion to a new computer system, policies, procedures, and corporate culture. Motivated bank staff and maintained morale by providing comprehensive training and addressing employee needs and concerns while personally completing extensive bank training.

- Monitor, disburse, and payoff consumer and commercial loans. Perform post-closing duties for residential and commercial construction loans. Prepare and submit loan packages to the Small Business Administration (SBA) for approval.

- Assumed management of trust department with $300,000 in assets. Effectively marketed trust department services and grew assets to $12 million in 5 years.

Communications

- Wrote, produced, financed, and directed *Resume Writing*, a 45-minute video guide to writing and producing effective resumes. Recommended in *Career News*, "...worthwhile guide to quickly writing a job-getting resume."

- Conceptualized, wrote, and edited *The Pressed Glass*, a monthly newsletter for the 2,000-member Antique Glass Association. Produced newsletter using desktop publishing.

- Designed and illustrated *Computer Life*, an 80-page, 4-color corporate magazine for the Computer Dynamics Corporation. Managed in-house production staff of 8 and 3 contract employees.

- Researched and assisted in writing *Stock Picks for 1996*, published by Business Books Press.

- Established a successful newspaper for the dental industry. Recruited industry experts to write columns, advertising, and develop direct mail campaign to dentists. Built circulation to 7,000 in one year with revenue of $80,000.

- Executed cablecasts of scheduled programming for four cable access television channels, one educational channel, and simulcast of one cable radio station on cable television.

- Completed sports, entertainment, and news reporting assignments for *Outside*, the campus newspaper for a 30,000-student university.

- Performed radio broadcasts for a weekly college radio show in a large metropolitan area. Acquired a technical expertise in radio production. Generated and maintained play lists.

- Planned and coordinated news releases, printed materials, and advertising for a professional accounting organization with over 250,000 national members. Contributed to a 10% membership increase by promoting organization through national and regional media.

- Designed and directed media campaigns on childcare for an early childhood development advocacy organization. Created media strategies and events; managed press listings and mailings. Collaborated with national organization in developing and sponsoring activities and programs, culminating in a celebration of "The Year of the Child."

- Generated international media attention for "The Hidden Spanish Treasure." Scheduled a 25-city, 4-country book tour including radio and television interviews, bookstore signings, and lectures at colleges, universities, and museums.

- Founding editor of *Computer World*, a monthly tabloid with circulation of 25,000. Directed the editorial and production of more than 2,000 pages a year. *Computer World* received 11 awards for editorial excellence during management tenure.

- Wrote scripts, edited, and produced videos for diverse professional associations. Supervised camera crews, editing staff, and clerical employees. Planned, budgeted, and managed video projects from inception to completion; produced quality products within tight deadlines, on time and within budget.

- Commentator for a weekly 90-second environmental commentary, "Safe World," WJJB-AM, morning and evening drive time.

- Host, "Cooking Healthy," a 30-minute taped cooking demonstration program aired weekly on a cable public access channel.

Computer

- Oversaw upgrade and maintenance of Data Processing Support Environment (DPSE) on a large-scale Ground Based Radar-Experimental software project (GBRX) consisting of 400,000 lines of executable code.

- Maintained life cycle documentation for GBRX including user manuals, system design description, and interface documents.

- Troubleshoot all state-of-the-art circuit technology. Monitor system activity and compile daily activity reports that measure the system's proficiency. Maintained life cycle documentation for GBRX including user manuals, system design description, and interface documents.

- Assemble, test, install, repair, and maintain end-user voice and data communications equipment and circuits for a local government contract. Troubleshoot communications circuits to diagnose voice equipment and circuit problems during the installation. Repair and replace faulty equipment; fabricate cables.

- Created complex technical specifications for changes/modifications to an on-line ordering system including client-server GUI-based applications running on Unix-based workstations, PCs, and terminals. Conducted detailed walkthroughs with developers and users; forwarded approved documentation to development for implementation.

- Managed data sharing between payroll, procurement, and personnel legacy systems and the centralized financial systems of a large computer manufacturer.

- Integrate, evaluate, and test HP 9000 series 700 and 800 minicomputers, IBM-compatible personal computers, and peripheral products on the Super-Minicomputer Program (SMP) contract. Peripheral devices include disk and tape drives, printers (laser, dot-matrix, and color), plotters, CD-ROMs, optical storage devices, RAID units, and FAX/modems.

- Design and implement standardized benchmark/evaluation criteria using DOS- and UNIX-based benchmark programs. Conduct system performance monitoring and tuning to determine optimum system configuration for customers.

- Standardize configuration for the HP-UX and SCO OpenDesktop operating systems, perform configuration management for shipping releases, and design automated installation processes.

- Enhance and maintain a COBOL- and VSAM-based payroll system. Prepare files, create and customize reports, and modify code as requested by public accounting officials. This system processes wages for worldwide employees.

- Devised a corporate methodology for delivering Information Engineering services. Developed procedures for using relational databases, consolidated data dictionaries, distributed databases, telecommunications, executive information systems, imaging, electronic document interchange, and system security.

- Developed system requirements for an on-line client-server Windows-based application to track user productivity in a nuclear power plant.

- Managed voice and data communications for small and large moves including analyzing, designing, planning, and installing. Coordinated all cable management, different circuit media and topologies, modular systems, closet layouts (distribution frames), and cabling infrastructure.

- Led a team in developing test tools and test scripts to perform end-to-end functional and performance tests of a telecommunications system.

- Maintained and upgraded a mechanized accounts payable system that processed bills payable to vendors and employee expense vouchers and calculated and produced reports to pay taxes of a Fortune 100 corporation.

- Provide analysis, programming, direction, and training for complete life cycle support for a vendor-based software package with over seven million lines of code (Vantage). Current project involves enhancements, support, and on call for a large mainframe system.

- Project manager for a successful conversion from a minicomputer to a super-mini computer. Supervised hardware and software conversion. Conducted analysis for project life cycle including hardware and software requirements. Completed project on time and within budget.

- Captured requirements and produced design for a major software re-engineering project utilizing Yourdon, CASE tools, and process and data modeling. Highly skilled in re-engineering legacy systems.

- Enhanced financial management system by designing and developing several custom report utilities coded in Pro*C with embedded SQL (Oracle 6.0).

- Assisted in the system conversion from DOS to MVS/XA and the implementation of a RACF security system for a Federal agency. Conducted daily security administrative functions, uncovered security exposures, and maintained Tape Library Management System (TLMS). Participated in developing and implementing disaster recovery policies and procedures. Performed daily production control maintenance.

Education

- Taught basic concepts in all curricular areas for grades 1 through 4 and social studies for grades 4 through 7.

- Worked with regular and special needs students from a variety of social and economic backgrounds including limited English-speaking students.

- Wrote language and social studies curriculum for grades 3 and 4 at an international school.

- Piloted new science program for grade levels 7 through 8.

- Taught third grade students. Team taught an inclusive writing workshop. Customized curriculum to utilize the computer lab to reinforce basic math and language arts skills. Implemented a grade-level thematic unit and successfully culminated with a program displaying children's projects.

- Created an individualized reading program for third graders. Increased student reading and writing ability through whole language, process writing, and varied forms of language expression. Provided intensive individualized instruction and adapted curriculum for borderline or failing students.

- Directed an elementary school music program. Taught grades 4 through 6 in the beginning and advanced band. Assisted students through private instruction.

- Conducted review sessions for undergraduate micro and macro economics courses; graded assignments and exams.

- Organized and supervised College Board Testing (SAT) and selected test administrators. Streamlined registration and administration.

- Head of the English department in a newly-established private boarding high school. Participated as team member in opening school; planned curriculum and department budget; selected and ordered textbooks.

- Taught Algebra to 75-95 seventh grade students. Created innovative curriculum that increased standardized achievement scores by 10% in first year.

- Student teacher for ten weeks. Assumed full responsibility for teaching United States History to 10th and 11th graders and Advanced Placement Government to 12th graders. Planned, organized, and executed lesson plans. Attended staff development workshops for high school teachers. Participated in parent-teacher meetings at the end of the grading period.

- Coached boys and girls track for grades 9-12. Oversaw 120 athletes, practices, and meets. Ordered equipment and uniforms; made purchases, inventoried equipment, and managed a $35,000 budget.

- Generated and implemented a variety of hands-on, developmentally appropriate lessons for a Kindergarten class of diverse five- and six-year-olds. Created innovative curriculum, tailored to meet the needs of all students, including one multi-handicapped child. Utilized various instructional styles including cooperative, open classroom instruction, and cross grade level teaching. Received outstanding evaluation.

- Tested and diagnosed high-risk, multi-cultural students in reading. Developed individualized reading and writing programs to meet student needs. Conducted workshops for parents and participated in evaluating and recommending services for children with learning and emotional problems.

- Taught a 6th grade class with 12 learning disabled (LD) students. Generated individual educational plans (IEP) and testing modifications. Instructed in all subject areas with a specialty in mathematics and language arts. Modified curriculum from mainstream classrooms.

- Applied a wide range of teaching methodologies to meet the individual needs of gifted and talented children in grade 4. Promoted active participation and enhanced broad educational experiences through creative presentations, resource materials, and a multitude of field trips.

Finance

- Planned and directed administrative cost accounting operations and budgeting functions for international health care insurance firm with 9 subsidiaries and revenue of $2 billion. Developed corporate budgets, prepared 5-year business plans; monitored and analyzed financial results. Identified financial problems and risks and recommended corrective action.

■ Managed financial operations of rapidly expanding national services corporation with sales in excess of $45 million. Directed profitable growth from $14 million to $45 million while reducing overhead costs.

■ Produced the monthly financial statements for one of the largest book publishers, detailing the actual, current, budget, and latest outlook financial positions.

■ Directed all new and used vehicle financing and leasing for a Mercedes Benz dealership. Doubled F & I gross profit from $190 to $390 per retail unit sold. Expanded department to include a second settlement officer and full-time aftermarket specialist.

■ Developed a corporate administrative budget over $210 million for an international health care insurance firm with revenues of $1.7 million. Managed a staff of 11 accounting professionals; recruited, hired, trained, and evaluated performance.

■ Ensured the accuracy of all general ledger accounts and provided accounting support for a 4,300-person, multi-division site of a large automobile manufacturer. Coordinated the annual budget process for the facility and prepared a $5 million operating budget.

■ Direct all financial and accounting operations for a paint manufacturer and retailer with 2 plants and 173 stores throughout 9 states. Manage accounting and financial reporting, financial planning and analysis, cash management and banking, credit, information systems, insurance, and administration of all retirement and health plans.

■ Managed financial operations of rapidly expanding national services corporation with sales in excess of $45 million. Directed profitable growth from $14 million to $45 million while reducing overhead costs.

- Design financial programs and improve cash flow for a commercial real estate development company with $82 million in holdings. Successfully negotiate corporate debt restructure projects totaling over $75 million in commercial loans with national and international banks.

- Direct a team of over 17 financial analysts in the monthly forecast of sales, earnings, cash flow, investment, and backlog for a $470 million subsidiary of an international corporation. Manage the results and brief the Division President and the Chief Financial Officer.

- Managed controllership functions of a rapidly growing $100 million equipment leasing company. Implemented financial controls and procedures which reduced external audit adjustments from $3.1 million in 1994 to zero in 1995.

Food Service

- Managed food service operation for high volume family restaurant with annual sales of $3.1 million and a staff of 45.

- Designed specialty items for the bakery department of a national grocery chain. Quality and quantity of work rated excellent.

- Initiated food utilization and portion control program resulting in a 7% reduction of food costs while maintaining quality and customer satisfaction.

- Planned, scheduled, and prepared meals for 190-seat steak and seafood restaurant.

- Directed the daily operations for restaurant in food pavilion. Hired and scheduled staff; ordered and inventoried food and supplies. Developed and managed budget; advertised and conducted public relations.

- Managed kitchen operations for a small upscale French restaurant. Ordered produce, developed daily specials, and wrote menus.

Supervised a staff of five. Effectively controlled costs and met sanitation requirements.

- Trained all servers on liquor, beer, and wine information in full-serving dining establishment. Maintained liquor costs and controls. Closed bar and restaurant.

- Performed server and host duties for high-volume restaurant. Greeted guests and maintained quality service.

- Direct all restaurant operations of medium-volume Mexican dinner house including profit and loss, employee staffing, training, and retention. Ensure quality control and guest satisfaction while maintaining the lowest personnel turnover in the Northeast Region.

- Coordinate wait staff for small restaurant. Prepare staffing schedules and resolve problems to ensure adequate coverage. Conduct weekly inventory of bar and food; maintain stock levels.

- Performed waiter duties for specialty steak house. Greeted customers and provided quality service. Helped with table set-ups and scheduling. Assisted as host.

- Manage all kitchen operations during dinner shifts, including grill and saute duties, for a newly-opened restaurant with a diverse menu.

- Direct operations of a full-service, casual dining establishment with annual revenue of $2 million. Manage a staff of 85 employees. Determine staffing requirements and qualifications; write and place employment advertisements. Conduct interviews, select employees; hire, train, and supervise. Review performance, counsel, and terminate employees. Conduct on-the-job training programs.

- Fill food orders for a small family restaurant. Check incoming food products for quality and freshness. Maintain rotating food stocks and ensure kitchen area conforms with Wisconsin Health Code Standards.

Health and Medical Services

- Worked for agency contracted to perform physical examinations for 14 insurance companies. Scheduled and conducted exams; documented pertinent information from client and exam, in compliance with individual insurance company policies.

- Managed organ donor program in the New York City metropolitan area from consent through the procurement process. Allocated organs, assembled surgical teams, and assisted in surgery. Conducted hemodynamic monitoring with pharmacologic and fluid interventions including central lines, swan ganz catheter, and ventilator management.

- Transcribe medical histories, physicals, consultations, operative reports, and discharge summaries for one of the largest national medical transcribing providers to local and out-of-state hospitals.

- Assessed, planned, and implemented therapeutic recreational programs within a children's residential treatment center. Completed patient assessments to determine motor skills, coordination, interests, and talents. Developed and proposed a treatment plan including goals, objectives, and therapeutic activities to be implemented by treatment team.

- Oversaw prevention and emergency care for 400-student elementary school. Conducted health screenings; identified at-risk students as member of Child Study Committee.

- Evaluated, developed, and conducted physical therapy treatment programs for geriatric home bound patients. Educated patients and family members.

- Implemented physical therapy treatment plans for outpatient, acute care, and long-term care patients. Informed patients of pathology and progress.

- Performed a full range of dental assistant responsibilities. Set up procedures and sterilized instruments; exposed and processed radiographs. Made and placed temporary crowns.

- Provide mental health treatment to adults, adolescents, children, couples, and families. Conduct outpatient psychotherapy to patients on medication as prescribed by psychiatrists and other physicians.

- Assisted patient with disabling head injury. Researched and designed home for the handicapped and coordinated home move. Investigated rehabilitation services and facilities. Hired and dismissed health care providers.

- Planned and directed speech services for a company that provided contract professional services to disabled adults in day treatment programs. Conducted patient diagnosis and evaluation of speech and language competencies; assessed skills, planned and directed implementation of communication goals, and evaluated individual progress with interdisciplinary team.

- Supervised a three-floor unit and approximately 46 clients participating in a drug and alcohol treatment program. Observed and documented client behavior during shift; reported hourly observations in log book. Handled after hour problems and emergencies. Provided ongoing client care, support, and structure.

- Arranged and coordinated health fairs for government and private industry. Provided hands-on services including individual body composition analyses and cholesterol screening; supplied information and guidance from the results.

Hospitality

- Managed an exclusive country club with three gourmet restaurants, three bars, catering operations, movie theater, and liquor store.

- Direct all operations of a private, 1,300-member club with 18 hole golf course, pro shop, tennis facility with 12 courts and indoor bubble, swimming complex, snack bar, recreation grounds, and club house with banquet and meeting rooms.

- Market and sell corporate meeting room space for a full-service luxury hotel with 11,000 square feet of meeting space.

- Manage housekeeping functions and laundry operations for a 355-room full-service, suburban hotel, processing 5 million pounds of laundry for 8 hotels and generating annual sales of $1.5 million.

- Complete marketing and sales responsibilities for 400-room luxury hotel with $15 million in annual sales. Position hotel and oversee direct sales effort for room, catering, and restaurant revenue. Manage a staff of 14.

- Launched sales and catering department in new upscale restaurant. Created innovative marketing strategies, developed menus; organized and managed private events. Hired and trained wait and bartending staff.

- Participated on committees of charity events for the American Cancer Society, American Diabetes Association, and American Red Cross. Planned events, solicited contributions, and organized volunteers.

- Established convention services department. Planned, developed, and executed all pre-convention, on-site, and post-convention activities and logistics for annual conventions of 1,150 attendees.

- Organized and managed all aspects of conventions and meetings including workshops, symposia, and exhibitions for organizations in the public and private sectors.

- Plan, execute, and arrange meetings and events for a luxury hotel including annual conventions, board meetings, social events, seminars, and retreats with 2 to 1,500 participants.

- Coordinated large conferences for 410-room luxury hotel. Developed relationships with corporations and non-profit organizations and built referral business. Prepared budgets, planned and supervised conferences. Created menus, organized all food and services, and followed-up to ensure client satisfaction.

- Provide consulting services for meetings, events, and fundraising functions. Plan budgets, negotiate hotel contracts; schedule daily events, recommend room arrangements, and propose meals and entertainment. Assist in on-site coordination of events, mailings, and registration.

- Manage all aspects of catering business including sales, operations, and administration of corporate and social events for up to 500 guests.

- Sold, coordinated, and supervised banquet and business meeting activities for a 300-room full-service hotel.

- Planned meetings for groups of 10 to 1,200. Selected and compiled potential locations and sites based on customer requirements and budget.

- Oversaw front office functions and staff of 80 for a 790-room flagship property including check-in/check-out, bell staff, switchboard, and concierge services.

- Effectively utilized computerized reservation system (CRSS) to manage and meet hotel rate and occupancy goals.

- Maintained hotel properties including a 350-room convention hotel and a 70-room small hotel with 18 classrooms and full-service restaurant. Managed a staff of 14.

Human Resources

- Directed all human resources functions for the 4th largest Hilton hotel, a 1,556-room convention hotel with $64 million in annual sales. Led a team of 12. Oversaw recruitment, benefits, affirmative action, payroll administration, career management, cultural diversity, training, coaching and counseling, employee discipline, performance evaluations, and employee health.

- Created and administered an outplacement program during the downsizing and restructuring of an international bank. Collaborated with management to address transition issues for remaining staff.

- Coordinated internship program for large law firm. Interviewed candidates as member of recruitment panel; selected and recommended applicants. Oversaw and mentored interns for 6-12 week durations.

- Expanded employee benefits program to include pre-tax dollars and cafeteria-style selection to reduce costs and increase employee satisfaction.

- Staffed a start-up engineering firm from an initial staff of 8 at inception to a team totaling 48 within the first year of operation. Wrote job descriptions, performance standards, procedural manual, and employee handbook.

- Managed compensation and benefits programs for an international telecommunications company with 550 employees. Oversaw administration of 401(k) plan, medical, dental, and tuition reimbursement.

- Selected 110 potential upper-level managers and guided their career development. Exceeded company's executive retention and advancement standards by an average of 7% over a 12-year period.

- Administer benefits and affirmative action programs. Ensure satisfactory employee relations by coaching, counseling, and providing ongoing career guidance.

- Direct suburban hospital recruitment program including screening, pre-employment testing, and orientation.

- Identify, qualify, and recruit technical professionals for a Fortune 100 telecommunications company.

- Established a compensation program for a start-up computer firm utilizing job analysis and point factor evaluation system.

- Developed, designed, and conducted training programs for adult learners on professional development, technical databases, and customer service strategies.

- Create, customize, and deliver workshops on stress related topics, inspiring participants to make changes that promote quality and enhance their lives.

- Drafted administrative job descriptions. Identified temporary staffing needs; coordinated temporary assignments, trained personnel, and monitored performance.

Human Services

- Direct and manage administrative, programmatic, and financial functions of a publicly funded career development/employment related agency for one of the nation's largest counties. Provide workshops, seminars, career counseling, and other services to county residents and employees.

- Selected to co-chair a statewide task force charged with improving work/family policies and practices. Supervised work/family training for over 150 managers and supervisors.

- Provide crisis intervention and emergency health services to elderly patients. Interact with county and state agencies, local hospitals, and community resources to link clients with appropriate services.

- Managed a regional nonprofit advocacy, education, and direct services agency. Doubled annual budget to $700,000 through contract negotiation, grant writing, membership development, and fundraising activities. Increased staff from 5 to 18 in 3 locations.

- Assist victims of sexual assault and domestic violence with problem solving and third-party reporting. Provide linkage to community resources and support systems.

- Monitor and update client welfare benefits. Conduct home visits, investigate income/assets, interview clients, and gather and verify data. Maintain files and prepare written documentation to meet state requirements.

- Received military personnel emergency intake requests from outside agencies. Notified service members of family emergencies and arranged travel. Set up a collection process for borrowed funds through direct deposit.

- Develop alcohol and drug abuse prevention programs for a local government. Coordinate resources and services in collaboration with health department, schools, police, alcohol and drug services, churches, civic groups, non-profits, and community businesses.

- Assist callers on 24-hour crisis intervention hot line. Work one-on-one with individuals in need of support or in immediate crisis. Identify emergency calls; facilitate referrals to appropriate staff and agencies. Track all calls through computerized reporting and telephone follow-up.

- Assigned and resolved cases to assist young families in procuring housing, medical assistance, and mental health counseling.

- Provided a stable environment and cared for abused children while their mothers participated in support group meetings.

- Determined eligibility of clients for public assistance programs in the state of Michigan. Scheduled and conducted interviews; identified and investigated cases of suspected fraud or over-payment.

- Manage the daily activities for a soup kitchen operating seven days per week, ensuring all state licensing requirements are met. Coordinate a volunteer staff of 30 and court ordered community service workers. Interact effectively with guests and the community.

- Increased funding and services for mentally disabled citizens by actively participating in an area-wide coalition and serving as an advocate with local and state officials on behalf of their needs.

- Coordinate services for 150 children and youth residents with profound/moderate/severe disabilities. Perform parent counseling, foster home placement, and sheltered workshop placement and evaluations. Supervise and train student social workers. Interface with community and mental health/mental retardation agencies and the media. Conduct presentations for sponsored groups including television and radio appearances.

- Assist social worker on child protective service cases by maintaining a relationship with the client and worker, ensuring clients are able to get to and from prescribed programs and treatments. Act as liaison between client, service provider, and social worker.

Law

- Established a law practice with a specialty in estate planning and trust and estate administration.

- Prepare and settle cases for insurance company clientele involving product liability, tort feasor liability, workers compensation, and personal injury.

- Provide a full range of legal services to civil litigation practice, representing American and foreign clients before Federal and state courts and administrative agencies.

- Participated in litigation preparation. Analyzed and summarized discovery documents for client involved in breach of contract suits against the United States Government.

- Lead counsel to large metropolitan transportation authority. Handle personal injury and employment law cases. Extensive litigation and jury trial experience involving third party liability issues.

- Represent clients in general litigation, insurance defense, environmental law, personal injury, workers compensation, and bankruptcy.

- Sole practitioner specializing in tax planning and real estate law.

- Analyze factual and documentary evidence, draft pleadings and affidavits; research and write memoranda and briefs on procedural, evidentiary, and substantive legal issues.

- Conducted a civil and criminal practice involving trial and appellate work in the Federal and state court systems. Immigration expert providing counsel to other attorneys throughout the state of New York.

- Counsel to financial institutions, corporations, and other entities in commercial lending transactions, workouts, and bankruptcies. Represent businesses in mergers and acquisitions, joint ventures, private placements of securities, debt financings, and general corporate/partnership matters.

- Mediated multiple disputes in the pre-litigation stage through the Los Angeles County Courts and through the Mediation Clinic at the University of California at Irvine.

- Enforce Federal government affirmative action legislation. Investigate allegations; draft and file civil complaints on behalf of the United States of America. Conduct pre-trial discovery, prepare pre-trial motions, and argue all motions before Federal courts. Settle and try cases.

- Create, manage, and close client files for a busy legal practice. Assist attorneys with research and trial preparation. Prepare and perform real estate settlements. Experience with personal injury claims, bankruptcy proceedings, and New York State court procedures. Proficient with Westlaw.

- Provide secretarial and administrative support to legal office of metropolitan newspaper. Draft and prepare documents, docket cases, and maintain law library. Track all phases of trademark and patent applications. Create and maintain legal and confidential files; type and proofread, sort and distribute mail. Arrange meetings and conference calls.

Law Enforcement/Security

- Provide security for Seattle, Washington headquarter facility of the largest worldwide credit union employing 2,500 at headquarters and 3,300 worldwide.

- Conduct security patrols and operate sensitive surveillance equipment within the command center to prevent equipment loss and assure employee and physical safety.

- Ensure the safety and security of the largest hospital in the Dallas/Ft. Worth area. Prevent instances of safety and security violations by systematically patrolling and inspecting facilities.

- Respond to major crime scenes to locate, document, and preserve physical evidence through visual examination, photography, and collection. Maintain the integrity of each piece of evidence.

- Conducted crime scene investigations for any death of a violent or suspicious nature (murder, suicide, industrial accidents, drug overdose, and fire deaths), sexual assaults, armed robberies, bombings, major arson fires, internal affairs, and police officer-involved shootings.

- Examined physical evidence collected by other police officers for latent prints. Protected and prepared the evidence for presentation in a court of law. Updated the unit on the latest trends in crime scene approach and the development of latent prints.

- Directed major investigations of white collar crime and counterintelligence cases including bank fraud and embezzlement, bribery, conflict of interest, and antitrust. Successfully achieved convictions while performing under extreme pressure.

- Investigated stolen auto cases. Coordinated a multi-agency task force responsible for the identification and arrest of individuals operating a major auto theft ring and the recovery of numerous stolen vehicles.

- Executed all tasks associated with first responder police services, general patrol duties, field training officer, and accident investigation.

- Coordinated criminal informant activities. Recognized informant opportunities, encouraged police officers to develop sources, and ensured adherence to the law and regulations.

- Successfully handled all phases of police patrol. Contributed to the development of a police promotional opportunity test and created an emergency response manual for Suffolk County.

- Supervised a squad of 12 police officers in the Madison Heights District. Coordinated the investigation and response to high-risk incidents and serious crime scenes.

- Enforce traffic and criminal laws. Intercede and resolve domestic disputes to avoid and defuse potentially violent confrontations.

- Train and evaluate new police officers in report writing, accident investigation, criminal law enforcement, and street survival.

Management

- Selected to fill branch manager position of temporary placement office. Recruited and trained an office staff of 5 and oversaw a temporary employee base of 260. Managed an annual budget of $210,000 involving salary administration, advertising, and office expenditures.

- Managed sales of automobile security systems, alarms, and upgraded sound systems. Supervised a staff of three. Hired, trained, evaluated performance; oversaw time reporting and sales logs.

- Planned, organized, and directed a medical record department for a managed care corporation. Oversaw medical and radiology records and data management. Administered an annual budget of $72,000.

- Managed small to large dental practices with 4 to 6 treatment rooms and staffs of 4 to 14. Oversaw personnel, payroll, accounts receivable, accounts payable, and overall office administration.

- Direct a staff of 70 to 80 employees. Recruit, hire, train, and supervise; determine staffing requirements and qualifications, write and place employment advertisements; conduct interviews and select employees. Review performance, counsel, and terminate staff. Conduct on-the-job training programs.

- Administered a new major account price plan for 25 accounts. Developed and presented a training program on complex contractual terms for senior-level customers, sales staff, and administrative personnel.

- Assumed management of newly-purchased service stations. Oversaw facility remodeling, staffed stations, purchased all supplies and equipment, and generated new business. Complied with OSHA and EPA regulations. Doubled service sales for both facilities in the first six months of operation.

- Managed busy downtown office building gift shop from initial opening to a profitable enterprise. Oversaw all operations to achieve maximum efficiency and optimal customer service levels.

- Supervised and scheduled front office staff at a 500-room condominium property. Improved service by initiating and developing a guest services training manual.

- Managed office operations for 4 weekly newspapers that expanded from a staff of 4 to 22 with a circulation of 50,000. Directed circulation and carrier staff of 38-48. Hired, assigned routes, and processed payroll. Billed subscribers and resolved subscription problems.

- Assumed diverse management responsibilities for daily operations of convention hotel food and beverage outlets. Provided coverage for the Beverage Manager, Restaurant Manager, and Room Service Manager.

Nursing

- Worked in a 52-bed medical unit as a primary care nurse with responsibility for 9-11 patients. Performed admitting and daily assessments. Communicated with physicians concerning patient needs and assisted with procedures.

- Provide health care in the home environment to post-surgical patients and clients with head injuries, birth defects, genetic disorders, and degenerating diseases. Assess clients, guide through physical therapy routines, teach health maintenance, and help with daily living activities.

- Directed and managed nursing department in a long-term care facility with a staff of 42. Hired, trained, scheduled, and dismissed staff. Established nursing standards and objectives. Developed a needs assessment for the 125 residents. Collaborated with recreational director and nutritionist to meet resident needs.

- Established support group for patients in drug and alcohol treatment. Developed, conducted, and monitored 12-step programs; coordinated medical, social, and community speakers and resources.

- Assisted in treatment services at a comprehensive infertility services clinic. Performed pre- and post-operative nursing care for male and female patients. Counseled patients; conducted patient teaching on medications, procedures, and conditions. Administered medications and assumed unit responsibilities in manager's absence.

- Scheduled home care visits and provided nursing care to patients recovering from cancer, bypass, and abdominal surgeries. Assessed patients and recommended community resources.

- Worked in a comprehensive addiction treatment unit. Set up and dismantled a chemical detoxification unit. Consulted with physicians, potential patients, and families regarding treatment. Handled unscheduled emergency admissions. Contributed to community resource file and made referrals. Maintained hotline, kept unit inventory, and ordered supplies.

- Conducted prenatal and postpartum checkups, SVE pap smears, and cultures. Performed family planning; prescribed birth control pills and

IUDs (including removal and insertion of IUDs). Taught prenatal classes to groups of 10-16 parents.

- Administered medications, IV infusions, and blood transfusions. Identified patient discharge needs and coordinated planning with health care personnel. Primary advocate for patient rights. Conducted family/patient teaching within hospital and prior to discharge.

- Managed the daily care and rehabilitated stroke and close head injury patients in a 60-bed trauma-neurology setting. Assumed nursing responsibilities, as needed, in pediatrics, infectious diseases, oncology, and dialysis. Supervised Marymount University nursing students.

- Staff member in Cardiac Catherization Lab. Assist with all types of diagnostic heart procedures including Valvular Studies and Right Heart, Left Heart, Right and Left Heart Catherizations. Provide primary care to catherization patients. Support Cardiologist while performing catheter insertion, wire manipulation, and intracoronary injection.

- Lend assistance to a busy metropolitan, high-volume acute surgical unit during eight-week assignment. Perform comprehensive primary care to cardiovascular, thoracic, and vascular surgery patients.

- Served as Charge Nurse for 30-bed Trauma Orthopedic unit and worked with orthopedic and trauma patients. Carried out and transcribed physician's orders in administering oral, intramuscular, and intravenous medications and treatments.

- Contributed staff support to a high turnover immediate care unit during 16-week assignment. Administered direct patient care to diverse geriatric population including liver failure, pre-liver transplant, GI bleeds, unstable diabetics, and renal failure.

- Performed internal medicine, pediatric, and urgent care nursing responsibilities in a managed care setting. Conducted triage functions. Administered IV Therapy and allergy, insulin, chemotherapy, and travel immunization injections. Handled EKGs, 24-hour halter application, and wound care. Accessed and updated computerized patient records.

- Cared for labor, delivery, postpartum, at-risk prenatal patients, and well and sick infants. Assisted doctors during exams, treatments, delivery, and cesarean sections. Informed, taught, and provided support to mothers and family members. Consulted with doctors for emergencies.

- Headed pediatrics and medical surgical units. Identified daily staffing needs and scheduled staff to meet patient requirements. Recruited, interviewed, hired, evaluated, counseled, and dismissed registered nurses and nursing managers. Prepared and implemented $1.8 million annual budget.

- Handled all phases of nursing responsibilities for severely ill newborns in a pediatric intensive care unit.

- Utilized the nursing process with individuals and groups and participated in treatment planning. Initiated problem-solving strategies with co-workers to facilitate quality patient outcomes; administered medications and coordinated lab work and treatments in compliance with hospital policies and procedures.

- Planned, developed, and implemented all aspects of Alzheimer/dementia programs for the largest long-term care facility in Maryland. Worked in geriatric center including 558-bed nursing care center, 500 apartments of independent and assisted living, and an ambulatory health care center.

Retail

- Assist in overseeing operations for a chain of seven card/gift stores. Evaluate individual store performance and productivity; visit stores, recommend and implement display changes, and train staff. Prioritize merchandising and promotional efforts and assist managers in resolving problems and improving sales revenue.

- Managed all aspects of 78,000 square foot store. Increased store volume and raised store's ranking among 110 stores from 65th to 25th in 1992.

- Efficiently and effectively planned and directed operations of the largest convenience branch store with annual sales of $22 million. Managed 7 supervisors and managers in Human Resources, Customer Service, Security, Cash Management, Supply, Engineering, and Movement of Goods.

- Managed a retail security department; apprehended 150 shoplifters and recovered $50,000 in 1994.

- Assisted customers, designed store windows, arranged merchandise, re-stocked shelves, and handled cash and charge sales transactions.

- Performed a wide range of sales duties for specialty lingerie retail operation. Created effective window and in-store displays, assisted customers in selecting and sizing merchandise, and communicated special requests and trends to management.

- Executed timely cash transactions for thousands of customers while maintaining an accurate cash drawer. Accounted for product inventory and monitored a team of three co-workers.

- Assisted in operating a men's casual clothing store in an upscale mall. Provided exceptional customer service by extensive product knowledge and willingness to persevere and satisfy customer needs.

- Opened new super bookstore on time and within two-month deadline. Worked 80- to 100-hour weeks to staff store and train over 100 employees. Ordered and installed store fixtures and merchandised entire store.

- Progressive promotions and increased responsibility providing retail support services to 11 specialty home furnishing stores. Conduct monthly visits; review store performance, train staff, and assist in displaying and positioning merchandise.

- Direct new store openings. Set up stockroom and selling floor; prepare inventory. Create window and floor displays that effectively promote merchandise. Train on site managers and staff. Meticulously prepare stores for Grand Opening, skillfully implementing opening celebrations.

- Supervised all aspects of retail store start-up including construction, inventory, recruitment, promotions, and Grand Opening.

Sales/Marketing

- Successfully promote grooming and personal care products in a 110-store territory in the Raleigh-Durham area. Consistently increase sales by securing superior promotional support, motivating stores to build effective displays, and ensuring proper product distribution and accurate pricing.

- Transformed a sales team operating at 92% of goal; developed team and attained 117% of goal.

- Penetrated numerous State agencies selling on-line business information services. Expanded the business 15% in 1992 and 25% in 1993 to achieve 123% of goal.

- Sold directory advertising for the Southern Connecticut division of NYNEX Directories. Established and generated new advertising markets, serviced and maintained existing accounts, and aggressively sold all products.

- Promoted after eight months to market and manage national copier programs to designated Fortune 500 companies. Signed three national accounts in the first two months and signed the largest designated account in the Northeast Region.

- Launched banquet and meeting services for a new convention hotel. Targeted a niche market including national and trade associations. Performed cold calls and hand-delivered hotel literature to convention and meeting planners.

- Successfully develop and implement marketing strategies in Northern California sales territory for Xerox copiers and facsimile machines. Build and maintain client base and customer loyalty through high quality service delivery.

- Penetrated a Massachusetts territory and generated a sales base of over 1,200 clients. Earned approximately $242,000 annually in commissions.

- Developed innovative marketing and sales strategies, increasing consumer product sales by 32% and pre-tax profit by 64% during tenure.

- Sold long distance services to large businesses. Generated new revenue and handled existing customer base. Achieved top #2 sales representative out of a staff of 32.

- Directed electrical supply product operations for a 14-state area. Marketed products and cultivated territory, increasing the number of accounts from 7 to 38.

- Generate new and retain existing business by utilizing effective selling techniques and providing quality customer service.

- Successfully market, write contracts, and close new home sales for a large New England home builder. Develop and implement marketing strategies. Build and maintain client base and customer loyalty through quality service.

- Increased sales revenue 24% by shifting company from product- to customer-oriented focus and establishing effective in-house training programs for sales and marketing staff as well as distributor sales force.

- Employ a broad range of closing techniques through knowledge of customer purchasing objectives. Utilize an expertise in financing options.

- Built client relationships and educated end users on plumbing product capabilities. Sold products through supply houses and a network of distributors; prospected through cold calling, trade shows, and industry events.

- Managed soft drink sales and distribution personnel for the grocery and convenience store segment including 6 sales representatives, 43 route men and helpers, a supervisor, and an independent marketing firm that provided sampling and merchandisers for major accounts.

- Opened new accounts and gained new product placements of beer and wine in restaurants and hotels. Maintained and supervised distribution.

- Direct sales and profit objectives for the 6th largest regional builder with over 340 units per year in sales and currently operating 8 subdivisions with 1,300 lots in the early development stage.

- Manage all aspects of home sales, from contract to settlement, with products ranging from low, entry-level to top-of-the-line, move-up. Prepare $2.4 million annual budgets.

- Sold fiber optic, endoscopic, and other surgical equipment in a 3-state territory. Grew annual territory sales from $190,000 to $352,000 by fostering and maintaining positive, professional relationships with surgeons and other hospital personnel.

- Effectively marketed cosmetic products to potential customers by analyzing and meeting customer needs, recommending products, persuading customers on product benefits, and closing sales.

Senior Executive

- Established a home-based remanufacturing business. Moved to new location within 2 years and expanded business to carry a full line of computer supplies and a printer repair service. Developed business to annual sales of $525,000. Increased staff to 8 employees; recruited, hired, trained, and supervised.

- Expanded operations and built a small, family-run fashion retailer into a multi-store regional chain. Managed four stores; recruited, hired, trained, and developed staff.

- Directed membership services and convention planning for a 110,000-member national association providing educational alternatives, peer support, and grass roots involvement.

- Total P & L responsibility for 2 operating companies generating over $19 million in sales. Devised and implemented a strategic operating plan that boosted return on capital from 7% to over 19% in 5 years.

- Pioneered the establishment of a channels marketing concept. Developed program; secured internal support, funding, and recruited and trained business partners. Added 30-65 partners annually, despite staff constraints. Built revenue to an excess of $375 million.

- Key participant in the development and implementation of an adult education program for the nation's 12th largest school district serving an adult population of 400,000. Created and coordinated courses; recruited, interviewed, hired, and supervised 40-72 instructors.

- Opened a chain of 11 jewelry stores. Built revenue to nearly $6 million in annual sales. Raised over $1.6 million in seed capital from banks and personal investments. Determined site selections through mall sizes, key tenants, and demographic studies pertaining to household income, age groups, and population cells.

- Manage multiple companies building upscale single family homes at 3 project sites with projected sales revenue of $49 million. Oversee simultaneous production projects, consistently meeting quality guidelines on time and within budget.

- Founded a corporation providing moving and storage services to government entities. Set up, managed, and grew organization from inception to annual revenue of $900,000. Oversaw office management, finance, insurance, personnel, payroll, sales, marketing, operations, and legal affairs. Coordinated labor pool of 140-290 temporary workers.

- Directed all delivery operations for a large retailer with 17 stores. Oversaw efficient scheduling of all deliveries within a 50 mile radius; ensured customer and quality standards were met through staff training and effective merchandise handling. Hired, trained, managed, and motivated a staff of 70.

Travel and Tourism

- Arranged, booked, and modified air travel and car rental reservations. Assisted customers with fare shopping and ticket sales. Issued and reissued airline tickets. Appeased customers and resolved problems with canceled and delayed flights.

- Managed commercial and retail accounts for independent travel agency. Handled domestic/international ticketing and reservations, package and individual tours, and cruises. Made rail, hotel, and car arrangements.

- Assisted corporate clients with domestic ticketing and reservations using Apollo computer system. Adeptly resolved problems while providing quality customer care.

- Promoted Canada as a travel destination to travel agencies and consumers through seminars, trade shows, on-site agency visits, and special events.

- Manage branch office, reservation center, and a staff of 10 for travel agency with $9.2 million in annual revenue. Handle domestic/international ticketing and reservations, package, and individual tours. Develop and conduct travel operations training seminars for staff members.

- Organized and reconciled boarded customers and closed flights. Completed paperwork for each flight, verifying number of passengers on the aircraft, unaccompanied minors, disabled and wheelchair passengers on board, and approximate time flight departed.

- Coordinated the gates and agents for the rush hour activity of a commuter airline with approximately 22 flights out of one gate within a one-hour period. Scheduled and made boarding, delay, and cancellation announcements for each flight. Cleared flights, determined passenger counts, and identified potential misconnects. Recommended initiatives to expedite flight boarding and departures.

■ Investigated and processed lost and delayed baggage claims. Successfully mediated and settled disputes, handling difficult situations and personalities with finesse.

■ Provided exceptional customer service to airline passengers. Efficiently handled emergency situations and received commendations and promotions.

■ Supervised a staff of 30-35 flight attendants. Ensured quality performance and adherence to safety regulations by conducting in-flight observations, assessing in-flight performance, updating procedures, training, and counseling staff.

■ Provide diverse assistance to tourists at county visitors center. Handle telephone, written, and in-person inquiries on attractions, accommodations, and activities. Book hotel reservations and plan one- to seven-day tours of the area based on visitor itinerary and interest.

■ Marketed time share resort vacations to travel agencies and customers. Generated product enthusiasm, motivated travel agents to improve product sales, and sold co-op advertising to improve visibility.

■ Conducted daily interactive presentations to all age groups on conservation and preservation of wildlife through narrations and demonstrations at a large metropolitan zoo.

■ Coordinated tours of a small modern art museum. Researched history of individual paintings and coordinated "Painting of the Day" lectures. Handled security functions ensuring safety of the art collections.

■ Promoted our heritage at a national park by educating the public on the value of protecting and preserving natural and cultural resources. Created written and visual materials enabling visitors to access and comprehend park resources. Maintained all museum objects located at sites within the park.

Accomplishments

Resumes that are result-oriented are most attractive to employers. Descriptive statements that demonstrate what you did, how you did it, and under what circumstances delivers a message that once you have contributed to one organization, you're likely to perform in the same capacity for another.

Begin your statements with verbs that connote accomplishment and achievement. The following list suggests effective words:

Achieved, added, attained, awarded, built, consistently, earned, grew, increased, piloted, pioneered, promoted, ranked, recognized, and selected.

Accomplishment Examples

- Facilitated rapid annual business growth of 15% despite a market shrinking 5% annually.

- Produced 110% of plan for 15 of the 17 eligible years.

- Assigned to clean up retail store operation with volume of $8.2 million that was without a store manager for 6 months. Significantly improved sales revenue with the initial 6 months.

- Launched an imaginative advertising campaign, generating an increase of $2.5 million in annual sales.

- Recognized as one of the top ten sales performers since 1990.

- Exceeded prior year's sales by 32% within the initial 9 months of tenure.

- Achieved top customer satisfaction ranking out of 75 offices.

- Oversaw the largest single day store sales of $652,000.

- Sold a $6.5 million account—the largest account in company history.

- Ranked in top 10 out of 60 sales representatives while attending college full-time.

- Assumed management of pediatric practice requiring reorganization. Contributed to increase of annual gross revenue from $650,000 to $790,000.

- Achieved 7-year average merchandise shrinkage of .7% with an industry average of 2.1%.

- Selected to lead a region requiring organizational restructuring. Successfully reorganized and increased annual revenue from $23 million to projected $39 million in 1997.

- Gained five new support contracts as a result of superior performance.

- Acquired the largest market share among cellular agents in central Iowa market.

- Saved $52,000 per year by instituting human resources policies and systems, cross training, and fluctuating shift hours.

- Challenged to pull together an administrative team after a major downsizing. Upgraded staff's performance levels, morale, and efficiency while participating in the initiation and implementation of marketing and sales strategies that improved profits from a fiscal loss to $14 million in 1995.

- Dramatically reduced a chronic delivery problem by introducing production stock management practices.

- Reorganized custom decorating division, significantly improving morale and fostering team work while increasing sales 24% over a 5-year period. Initiated and implemented a collection system resulting in an average collection rate of approximately 95%.

- Instrumental in selecting product niches resulting in rapid, profitable growth.

- Achieved a 3% increase in annual sales, 4% greater than total ready-to-wear, despite company's Chapter 11 filing during this period.

- Efficiently managed a major downsizing of area stores, effectively maintaining morale and sales in the remaining stores. Oversaw acquisition of eight stores, liquidation of six, and closure of four.

- Restructured organization, downsizing staff by over 18% while increasing sales 25%.

- Invited to attend The Honorable Gerald L. Baliles Governor's Conference in Richmond, Virginia, "Child Care—Everybody's Business."

- Successfully weathered the New England economic downturn of 1990-1991.

- Improved profitability 5% during a turn-around period while maintaining high customer satisfaction.

- Succeeded despite lack of first line management resources, significant new hires, and almost total reassignment of personnel duties.

- Operated under budget during a 14-month period.

- Achieved sales performance never before attained.

- Contributed to continual profitability of organization despite turbulent economic environment.

- Increased group revenues 25% and food and beverage profits 17% despite a soft market.

- Promoted to manage flagship mall location, the largest branch in a national retail chain.

- Pioneered "City Service" concept; the purchase and rental of vehicles that met big city requirements. Effectively marketed program resulting in adoption nationwide.

- Broke all sales records in 1995. Quadrupled sales revenue in a three-state territory.

- Consistently rank in top 4 out of 100 most productive accounts nationwide.

- Nationally selected from over 13,000 applicants to participate in the living, working, and learning experience of the Walt Disney World College Program.

- Developed unprecedented customer loyalty and retention by anticipating needs and eliminating surprises.

- Achieved #3 ranking out of 40 after initial year.

- Tripled sales revenue in the initial year by establishing strategic relationships in all customer segments. Employed a diverse marketing mix appropriate to the sell cycle stage including mass mailings, database marketing, fax specials, advertising, trade shows, and cold calls.

- Managed store operations transforming store performance from a loss to the most profitable one in the 21-store chain.

- Completed rigorous six-month training program finishing second in class.

- Recognized in June 1994 as the first account executive in the company's history to invoice in excess of $235,000 in one month.

- Maintained the lowest personnel turnover in a chain of 66 fast food restaurants.

- Maximized cash flow during period of illiquidity through aggressive cash management.

- Selected by ABC network as a quality customer service-oriented facility and featured on a network program.

- Saved company money and reduced filing by implementing paperless purchasing.

- Built a successful sales staff by hiring and training five sales executives, four who rank in the top 5% nationwide and one currently #1 nationwide.

- Achieved Master Teacher, Career Level II, Dade County Public Schools, 1986.

- Doubled revenue base in Nashville office within the first six months.

- Completed a re-invention and re-engineering of the Federal Division; streamlined organization 17% from 9,000 employees to 7,470.

- Increased gas sales at Highview Mobil from 72,000 gallons per month to 245,000.

10 Tips for Crafting Your Work History

1. Job seekers often find the experience section the most difficult to write. Begin at the beginning. Outline all of your work experiences, both paid and non paid. Volunteer experience is important and it may strengthen your credentials.

2. Start with the most recent experience first and work backwards. Include the job titles, organization names, city, state, and dates of employment.

3. List all of your work responsibilities for each job. Quantify wherever possible. Did you manage a staff of 2 or 10? Did you administer a budget of $110,000 or $13 million?

4. Identify what you accomplished in each job. What did you contribute or do differently that wasn't done before?

5. Begin each job with a statement that indicates your primary responsibility, for example, "Directed a worldwide operation marketing telecommunications equipment to Federal civilian agencies."

6. Connect and group like statements together. Look for balance in the length and appearance of your paragraphs.

7. Try setting off your experience statements with bullets. Both round and diamond-shaped bullets can effectively highlight your action verbs and statements.

8. Edit and rewrite your sentences using concise statements. Make it easy for employers to read your resume with fewer words and clear, uncluttered sentences.

9. Highlight your accomplishments by placing them after your responsibilities. You can showcase significant achievements by centering a subtitle, "Selected Accomplishments," or "Accomplishments and Achievements" and follow with bulleted accomplishments.

10. Demonstrate progression and added responsibility by beginning statements with "progressive promotions from" or "promoted to."

Action Verbs

abstract	anticipate	attain
accelerate	apply	audit
achieve	appoint	author
acquire	appraise	automate
adhere	approve	book
adjust	arrange	brief
administer	assemble	budget
advance	assess	build
advise	assign	canvass
advocate	assist	capture
analyze	assume	chair
answer	assure	check

classify	develop	head
close	devise	hire
coach	diagnose	host
co-author	direct	identify
collaborate	dispatch	illustrate
collect	distribute	implement
communicate	diversify	improve
compare	document	incorporate
compete	downsize	increase
compile	draft	inform
complete	edit	initiate
compose	educate	inspect
conceive	employ	install
conceptualize	enable	institute
conciliate	encourage	instruct
conduct	enforce	integrate
configure	enhance	interact
confirm	enlarge	interface
consolidate	ensure	interpret
construct	establish	interview
consult	estimate	introduce
contact	evaluate	invent
contract	exceed	inventory
contribute	execute	investigate
control	expand	invite
convert	facilitate	issue
coordinate	file	justify
counsel	finalize	launch
cover	finance	lead
create	forecast	lend
cultivate	formulate	liaison
customize	foster	litigate
decrease	fulfill	locate
define	furnish	lower
delegate	gather	maintain
deliver	generate	manage
demonstrate	grow	manipulate
design	guide	market
determine	handle	match

maximize	raise	spearhead
mediate	rank	stabilize
meet	recognize	streamline
merge	recommend	strengthen
modify	reconcile	submit
monitor	record	substantiate
motivate	recruit	succeed
negotiate	re-design	summarize
observe	reduce	supervise
obtain	re-engineer	supply
offer	regenerate	support
open	re-invent	surpass
operate	release	survey
orchestrate	re-negotiate	teach
order	reorganize	team
organize	repair	test
orient	replace	testify
originate	represent	track
oversee	research	train
participate	resolve	transcribe
perform	restructure	transform
pilot	retain	transmit
pioneer	retrofit	transport
place	revamp	treat
plan	revise	typeset
possess	route	update
prepare	run	utilize
present	satisfy	validate
prioritize	save	verify
process	schedule	work
procure	screen	write
produce	secure	
promote	select	
propose	sell	
prospect	serve	
provide	service	
publicize	settle	
publish	set up	
purchase	solve	

4

Education Enhancers

The education section of your resume demonstrates your development and training; where you formally acquired knowledge and capabilities and cultivated your skills through instruction and study. It should include all post-secondary degrees, certificates, and diplomas from junior colleges, four-year colleges and universities, professional and technical schools, and professional and certificate programs. Indicate school name, city, state, completion date, and major/minor course of study.

If you've achieved academic honors, include Dean's List, graduation with distinction, summa cum laude, magna cum laude, scholarships, awards, and a high class ranking. Only recent college graduates list grade point averages (G.P.A.).

Need more pizzazz? Consider stating how much you financed your education or internships/externships, thesis, or class projects that demonstrate how you meet job requirements.

Qualification Boosters

Use the education section to bolster your qualifications and maximize your credentials by including professional development through workshops, seminars, conferences, and courses sponsored by professional organizations, corporations/governments, educational institutions, and private training companies. Include training and professional development provided by your employers.

Lacking College Degree?

Don't despair or count yourself out of the running if you didn't go to college or attended college, but didn't complete a degree. You have probably acquired skills by attending workshops or job-specific training.

If you have attended college but did not complete a degree, include the information and state what you achieved. If you are currently attending college but have not yet completed, you can state you are pursuing a degree and when you anticipate completion.

10 Tips for Developing Education Entries

1. Either spell out or abbreviate college degrees. Make your choice based on available space and how the information fits best on the page. Whether you choose to abbreviate or not, be consistent with all your degrees.

2. Which is more impressive, your degree or educational institution? Decide which you'd like to emphasize and either place first, use uppercase, or highlight with bold.

3. Do you feel that including dates for the year you received degrees, diplomas, and certificates may reflect your age and cause age discrimination? Be aware that omitting completion dates may cause an employer to suspect that you are even older than you actually are.

4. If you have attended the same college for more than one degree or course of study, indicate the college first and organize the degrees together, beginning with the most recent.

5. Make this section more descriptive by including majors, minors, concentration, and courses of study. You can eliminate majors if they have no relationship to your career objective and could potentially hamper your ability to land a job.

6. Avoid including high school if you have any training or post-secondary education.

7. If you have attended a number of educational institutions to complete your degree, you do not have to include them all. Indicate the educational institution that awarded your degree, the degree, and date of graduation.

8. Recent college graduates use the month and year a degree was received. Include just the year if you are not a recent graduate.

9. If you have an associate and bachelor degrees you can include them both or just your bachelor degree. If you have bachelor and masters degrees they both should be included. If you have an associate, bachelor, and masters, include just the bachelor and masters.

10. If education does not strengthen your credentials, downplay this area with the section title. While Education is the most often used title for this section, you can effectively use Training, Professional Development, or Education/Training.

College Graduate Examples

B.A., Political Science, minor in Business Marketing, 1994
Shaw University, Raleigh, North Carolina

Bachelor of Arts in English, 1981
George Mason University, Fairfax, Virginia

Master of Science in Accounting, 1980
American University, Washington, D.C.

Bachelor of Arts in Economics, 1970
State University of New York, Geneseo, Geneseo, New York

Psychiatric Residency, Columbia University Medical School, New York, New York

Medical Internship, Washington Hospital Center, Washington, D.C.

M.D., University of Virginia, Charlottesville, Virginia

B.S. in General Studies, Tulane University, New Orleans, Louisiana

College Graduate Combinations Examples

Northeastern University, Boston, Massachusetts, **J.D.**, 1985, **B.A.**, 1982

Brown University, Providence, Rhode Island
   Masters in Business Administration, Finance, 1972
   Bachelor of Science, Industrial Engineering, 1968

     UNIVERSITY OF VIRGINIA, Charlottesville, Virginia
MASTER OF SCIENCE with honors, Nursing Administration and Adult Mental Health, 1992
BACHELOR OF SCIENCE, Nursing with specialty in Administration, Care of Adults, and Pediatrics, 1988

HARVARD UNIVERSITY, Cambridge, Massachusetts
Bachelor of Architecture, 1971, **Bachelor of Science**, 1970

College Graduate with Honors Examples

Bachelor of Science in Civil Engineering, graduated with honors,
Loyola College, Baltimore, Maryland, 1979
Intermediate honors, Chi Epsilon, Civil Engineering Honor Society

Montana State University, Bozeman, Montana
   B.A. in English, 1974
   President of Student Government; selected by faculty and students for "Outstanding Student Award"

Westchester County Criminal Justice Academy, White Plains, New York
   Basic New York State Law Enforcement Training course, 1987
   Ranked first in academy class

Bachelor of Science in Nursing, St. Mary's College of Maryland, St. Mary's City, Maryland, 1990
  Athletic Scholarship Funding, St. Mary's College of Maryland Varsity Track Team

Masters in Business Administration, Top 10 in Class, University of Arizona, Tuscon, Arizona, 1994

Penn State University at Harrisburg, Harrisburg, Pennsylvania
  J.D., 1985. Graduated in top 10% of class. Associate Editor, Penn Law Review, 1984-1985.

Bucknell University, Lewisburg, Pennsylvania, **B.S. Hotel Restaurant and Institution Management, magna cum laude**, 1988
  Rhodes Scholar nominee, athletic and scholastic scholarships, Peter A. Smith Memorial Award, American Hotel Foundation Merit Award Winner

Bachelor of Science, Economics, 1990
  Colgate University, Hamilton, New York
  Received *Certificate for Outstanding Scholarship*, 1989, 1990

Citrus College, Glendora, California
  Associate in Applied Science, Physical Therapist Assistant, 1993; nominated for **Citrus College Clinical Excellence Award**, Spring 1993

Bachelor of Arts, History, Government, Economics, Phi Beta Kappa, Dakota State University, Madison, South Dakota, 1987

Cornell University, Ithaca, New York
  Bachelor of Science in Mathematics, minor in Education, 1994
  Recipient, Moore Award for Innovation in Education

Bachelor of Science, Grand Valley State University, Allendale, Michigan, 1995; Full tennis scholarship; All American—1993

Quincy College, Quincy, Massachusetts
> **Bachelor of Science in Industrial Engineering, graduating with distinction in humanistic studies**, 1976

United States Air Force Academy, Colorado Springs, Colorado
> **Bachelor of Science in Applied Science**, 1993
> Graduated with Honors, Brigade Honor Board, Class Secretary

B.S. in Business Administration, Marketing, Taylor University, Upland, Indiana, 1988
> Top third of class; earned 90% of college expenses; College Football, Championship Team, Linebacker

St. Lawrence University, Canton, New York
> **B.S. in Management**, 1987. Dean's List. Financed 100% of education.

Certificates/Diplomas Examples

Travel and Tourism Diploma and **Bartending Certificate**, Durham Technical Center, Durham, North Carolina, 1990

INTERNATIONAL BROTHERHOOD OF ELECTRICAL WORKERS (IBEW), Washington, D.C.
> **Internationally Recognized classification of Journeyman Wireman; completed courses in Five-Year Electrical Apprenticeship Program**, May 1996

Virginia Merit Shop Education Foundation Inc., Arlington, Virginia
> Completed four years of electrical studies, September 1996
> Certificate of Completion, Electrician Apprenticeship of 48 months, Commonwealth of Virginia, September 1996

Certificate, Purchasing Management, Pace University, New York, New York, 1995

Travel Specialist Program, Certificate of Completion, Grey Travel School, New Orleans, Louisiana, 1990

Certificate of Completion, Eunice Business College, Eunice, Louisiana, 1988

Life Office Management Association (LOMA)
Associate Customer Service (ACS) Certification, 1996
Pursuing **Fellow Life Management Institute (FLMI) Certification**

Certificate, Human Resources Management, American University, Washington, D.C., 1993

Henry Miller Academy, Aberdeen, South Dakota
Diploma, Business Secretary, Computer Operations/Word Processing Specialist, 1988

Control Data Institute, Arlington, Texas
Graduated 1982 with 750 hours of individualized instruction in Computer Technology. Courses included Basic Electronics, Introduction to Computer Systems, Central Processor Hardware and Software, and Peripheral Equipment.

Pursuing Education Examples

Bachelor of Arts, English, Cameron University, Lawton, Oklahoma, anticipate Summer 1997

Anticipate **B.S., major Business Administration**, Azusa Pacific University, Azusa, California, Fall 1997

Monroe Community College, Rochester, New York
Pursuing business pre-requisites and will transfer to State University of New York College at Geneseo, Geneseo, New York to complete B.S.
A.A.S., Architectural/Construction Technology, 1995
Maintained a 3.5 G.P.A.

College of Financial Planning, Denver, Colorado
Pursuing Certification as a Financial Planner

Pursuing **Bachelor of Science, Political Science**, Oklahoma State University, Stillwater Oklahoma; require 25 credit hours for completion

Anticipate graduating with a business degree from Malone College, Canton, Ohio; completed three years of course work at Ohio University, Athens, Ohio

SUNY COLLEGE AT POTSDAM, Potsdam, New York
   Pursuing **Bachelor of Science in Recreational Management** in one of the most respected programs in the United States

Training and Professional Development Examples

Audited **Administrative Justice** course, Austin Community College, Austin, Minnesota, Fall 1996

Professional Development: Learning Tree; completed *PC Troubleshooting and Configuration* (Certified) and *LAN Troubleshooting*. Scheduled for *Local Area Networks* and *ISDN*.

Xerox Corporation Management Training
   Management Studies, New Manager Seminar, Managing for Motivation, Management Action Workshop

Language and Cultural Experience Studies
   Hungarian Language Institute, Budapest, Hungary, Summer 1996
   Pontifica Universidad Javeriana, Santa Fe de Bogota, Columbia, 1994-1995
   University of the Andes, Merida, Venezuela, Winter 1993

Professional Development
   Numerous courses in Sales and Management, Image and Fashion Training, Recruiting and Promotion Skills

Extensive banking and computer training, American Institute of Banking, Washington, D.C.

Professional Development at Chase Manhattan Bank
Accounting I and II, Managing People, Sales Management, Consumer Lending, Mortgage Lending, Series 6 Brokers License, Financial Statement Analysis, Commercial Business Development, Time Management

Computer Training
Completed basic courses in Excel, Word, PowerPoint, Harvard Graphics

Professional Development
Attended numerous workshops in Successful Sales Techniques

Fashion Seminars
Girbaud, Guess?, Michael Yacobian Selling Techniques, Macy's Vendor Seminars

Victim Assistance Network (Arlington County, Arlington, Virginia)
Completed 40-hour training program in crisis intervention involving sexual assault and domestic violence

Computer Systems Applications Program, Shorter College, Rome, Georgia Extension, 1987
Courses in Joint Application Design (JAG) Facilitation Workshop, Imaging, Business Process Redesign, Information Engineering-Rapid Application Development, Data Resource Planning, Data Communications, Novell Netware Service and Support, Novell Advanced Netware Systems Manager, Novell Netware Systems Manager, Intermediate UNIX Seminar, C language, Advanced Troubleshooting, and PC Repair.

Professional Development at Marriott International, Inc.
Total Quality Management II — Problem Solving
Certified Quality Trainer in Total Quality Management I
Supervisory Training
Training Skills I and II

Professional Training
C **Programming**, 40 hours, Computer Training Associates, 1991
DEC/VMS Operating System, 80 hours, ATV Computer Corp., 1991
Oracle RDBMS, 40 hours, Wilson Computers, 1988

Incomplete Education Examples

NORTHERN VIRGINIA COMMUNITY COLLEGE, Alexandria, Virginia
Completed 45 hours towards an Associate in Applied Science in
Business Management

Completed 135 credits towards a **B.S., Information Systems, Business
minor**, Vanderbilt University, Nashville, Tennessee

Courses in personal computers; extensive Bell System and AT&T company
schools spanning over 25 years of service; completed three years at Oregon
State University, Corvallis, Oregon.

Salem State College, Salem, Massachusetts
Three courses required for completion of **M.Ed in Counseling**

Completed 22 hours of graduate courses in Writing, Education, and French,
University of Virginia, Falls Church, Virginia and Georgetown University,
Washington, D.C.

Pace University, New York, New York
Completed two and a half years towards a Bachelor of Science in
Business

Graduate studies in Marketing, Case Western University, Cleveland, Ohio

Evergreen Valley College, San Jose, California
Course work in Computer Science

Completed 43 credits towards Associate in Applied Arts, Mattatuck
Community College, Waterbury, Connecticut

Lindenwood College, St. Charles, Missouri
Completed studies in **Public Relations** and **Communications**, 1983-1985

International Brotherhood of Electrical Workers, Chicago, Illinois
Completed two years of Electrician Course, 1979-1980

5

Skill Builders

A skill is the ability to effectively perform a task or activity. You are not born with skills; they are developed and learned, based on knowledge, know-how, and specialized subject matter.

Acquiring skills takes discipline, motivation, and time. Skills aren't cultivated simply by attending workshops or training programs. Expertise is gained by studying, practicing, and applying the information.

Skills that merit inclusion in a separate section demonstrate special knowledge and technical ability acquired in formal settings such as colleges, universities, vocational and technical schools, continuing education, apprenticeship programs, on-the-job, or company/organization training. While computers, foreign languages, communication, equipment, technical, and mechanical proficiencies are most often included, any skill that demonstrates that you satisfy job requirements can be mentioned.

Skill Levels

It's helpful to use descriptive markers that indicate the ability level of your skills.

- **Knowledge** suggests practical ability or skill, information or understanding acquired through experience.

- **Proficiency** demonstrates that you are thoroughly adept and versed.

- **Expertise** implies the knowledge, skills, or experience of an expert, a specialist with unique skills or knowledge.

10 Tips for Showcasing Your Skills

1. Place this section where it will have the most impact. Are your skills highly sought and desirable? If so, consider including this section right after your summary. If your skills are strong but not a key factor in your overall experience, place this section after either experience or education.

2. Be descriptive by naming the types of computer equipment, software, and languages.

3. Describe your skills by indicating the levels of knowledge and experience.

4. If you have extensive computer knowledge, you may want to include separate sections for computer software, applications and languages, CASE tools and information engineering, databases, voice and data communications, operating systems and platforms, and hardware.

5. It's important to accurately spell the names of software. If in doubt, check the software package or manual or look up advertisements in computer magazines.

6. State your knowledge level of each foreign language. Fluency indicates you are capable of speaking or writing with effortless ease while native language demonstrates a fluency that is linked to you by birth.

7. Choose conversant if you are well acquainted or familiar with a

language through study or indicate speak and/or write or speak and understand to clarify your language ability.

8. Identify typing or shorthand (transcription) speed for positions that require this skill.

9. If relevant, include types of office equipment.

10. Integrate your skills applications into experience sections so employers can see how it applies. For example, "Create customized spreadsheets using Microsoft Excel" or "Translated hotel guest guide from Spanish to English."

Computer Examples (for 2 Individuals)

- **Programming Languages**: Microsoft Basic, SQLPLUS, HTML (Internet).
  Software: Paradigm Plus, Microsoft Word, Microsoft Excel, Microsoft Draw, Windows, Visio, Netscape, Mosaic, WordPerfect.
  Hardware: IBM PC and Macintosh systems; DOS and Unix operating systems.

- **Hardware:** Comprehensive knowledge of computer system architectures and computer-related devices. Provide full system support (installation, integration, configuration) for IBM and compatible personal computers, Sun Microsystems' servers/workstations, and Hewlett Packard Series 9000 minicomputers/workstations. Evaluate, integrate, and troubleshoot a wide variety of peripheral devices including modems, scanners, printers, data storage, CD-ROM/optical storage, and X-terminals.
  Software: DOS, SCO XENIX, SCO UNIX Open Desktop (ODT), Sun OS, HP-UX, OS/2, Novell Netware 3.11, Windows 3.x, and Windows NT. Expertise with software applications including word processors, spreadsheets, desktop publishing, graphics, presentation, personal information managers, document imaging and storage, electronic mail, financial management, memory managers, system utilities, and imaging applications. Install, maintain, and provide end-user support.

Networks: Experienced in the installation, configuration, and day-to-day operation of Local Area Network (LAN) equipment and related software. Knowledge of network concepts including design, layout, protocols (TCP/IP, IPX, etc.) and services (NFS, NIS, etc.). Expertise with installing, maintaining, and troubleshooting telecommunication hardware including routers, hubs, bridges, and modems.

Technical Skills (for one individual)

- **Systems Development:** Networking (3COM/XNS, Novell/IPX, UNIX/TCP/IP, DEC/DECNET), IBM/SNA Network, Appletalk Network, Video Network, Satellite TVRO (VSAT), Video Teleconferencing (VTC), Multi-site Connectivity, Security Call-Back, Voice Mail, Microwave System, Voice Services, Packet Switching.
  Technical Support: Trouble Shooting/Diagnostics, Power Protection, Hardware Installation/Connectivity, Wiring Systems/Components.
  Hardware: AT&T, IBM, DEC, HP, SUN, Apple, 3COM, Cabletron, CODEC, 10 Base T Hubs, DSU/CSUs, Controllers, VTC, VSAT, Transceivers, Bridges, Repeaters, Terminal Servers, Multiplexers, Routers, Modems, Concentrators.
  Circuit Media: Thin/Thick Coax, Fiber Optic, UTP, Microwave, Satellite, CATV Cable, Plant (Exchange) Cable, T1s, Dedicated Leased Circuits (1MB, 1ML, 4-WIRE, T1s).

Equipment/Mechanical/Technical Proficiency Examples

- Typing, 70 wpm, Shorthand, 90 wpm; proficient with Microsoft Word and WordPerfect; skilled with Lotus 1-2-3 and Microsoft Excel; familiar with Pagemaker.

- Proficient with all general office equipment including computers, WordPerfect, Peachtree Payroll, and Microsoft Excel.

- **Technical:** Blueprint Drafting and Reading, Site Planning, Working Drawings, Ditchwitch and Backhoe Operations.
  Computer: CADD Operations, IBM PC, Lotus 1-2-3, WordPerfect.

- **Construction Skills**: Highly skilled and experienced in framing with wood or metal studs, drywall installation and finishing, insulation, interior/exterior painting, concrete pouring and finishing, minor electrical wiring (lights, switches, and plugs), ceramic tile and marble installations, operating skid-steer loaders and forklifts, and installing metal and PVC conduit.

Language Examples

- Fluent in Spanish; strong understanding of Latin cultures from living in Ecuador, South America.

- Conversant in French.

- Fluent in French (native), English, and German.

- Fluent in Tagalog; moderately fluent in Spanish and Italian.

- Fluent in Spanish and English. Lived and attended school in Mexico City for over ten years. Assisted Spanish teachers in high school and college in correcting tests and papers; tutored classmates in Spanish.

- Fluent in Spanish and proficient in French.

- Fluent in spoken and written Spanish and English.

- Moderately fluent in German.

- Five years of French; conversant in Spanish; extensive international travel.

6

Extra Credits—
Awards, Honors, Certifications, Licenses, Professional Affiliations, Publications

Awards, honors, certifications, licenses, and publications all reflect effort, commitment, and demonstrate success and accomplishment. Membership in professional organizations implies involvement and participation as well as a sincere interest between you and your chosen occupation.

Awards and Honors

Awards and honors illustrate achievement that is earned, won, or awarded through superior performance. They are based on independent, team, group, or organizational performance or competition and awarded by private, public, academic, and non-profit organizations, foundations, industries, professional affiliations, alliances, and societies.

Appointments or elections convey leadership or recognition of superior skills or performance.

Nomination, selection, or finalist for an award is an honor too, even if you didn't reach the very top. Any recognition of your performance is an achievement.

Employment awards and honors include outstanding/exceptional performance appraisals, performance awards, letters of commendation, letters of appreciation, and monthly, quarterly, annual organizational achievements.

Industry and professional honors include selection for awards that recognize individual, team, or organizational achievement based on a product or performance.

Educational honors can be grouped in either the honors/awards or education section. List scholarships, fellowships, selection to honor societies, sororities, or fraternities, and scholastic recognition.

Examples

- Bachelor of Arts with honors, ranked in top 20% of class, 1991.

- Passed CPA exam on first sitting.

- Awarded Graduate Research Fellowship, Stanford University, Stanford, California, 1995.

- Appointed and served on extensive boards and commissions in the areas of telecommunications, education, civic issues, and advocacy.

- Recipient of Scholastic Excellence Award.

- Honored with the "Golden Fork Award of New England" for five years.

- Selected "Man of the Year," 1988.

- *Gifted Student Guide* nominated for "Young Parents Book Award."

- Commended for performance of wiring and piping life safety and emergency systems at Community General Hospital in Des Moines, Iowa.

- Recognized as "Salesman of the Year," 1992.

- "Branch of the Quarter Award Winner," 1995.

- Achieved #2 in company, 1990.

- "Quality Award," selected for three quarters 1994, two quarters 1995.

- Received numerous letters of customer appreciation.

- Selected "Regional Manager of the Year" and achieved 125% of quota, 1995.

- Awarded "Sales Leader of the Month," June 1990, September 1991, May 1992, August 1993.

- Attained six years of "Quota Club."

- Cash awards and incentives, ranging from $100 to $20,000, awarded for different achievement levels.

- Received four achievement awards for team and report writing contributions.

- Honored as #1 Rep in Region, 1st and 3rd quarter, 1994.

- Received "Army Achievement Medal for Superior Performance."

- Selected as 1993 "Director of Sales of the Year."

- Received "ABC Information Services Award," in recognition of contributions to profitability, quality, and excellence within information systems, January 1995.

- Selected for *Who's Who Among Rising Young Americans*.

- American Hotel Foundation Merit Award Winner.

- Lifetime Member Phi Kappa Sigma Honor Society.

- Rhodes Scholar Nominee.

- Received "Letter of Commendation" for outstanding performance from Ms. Regina Wilson, Regional Vice President and Ms. Katharine Ash, General Manager.

- Won national awards for two consecutive years for achievements in revenue/pre tax objectives.

- "Leadership Club," selected eight times for exceeding all assigned objectives.

- Recipient of the "Italian-American Cultural Award" presented by the Romano Foundation, New York, 1984.

- Awarded "The Klinger Prize in Science" at the Massachusetts Institute of Technology, 1976.

- New York State, "Meritorious Award," 1988.

- Awarded incentive trip for excellence as a Regional Education and Service Manager, 1993.

- Millionaire Club Winner, 1986.

- International Who's Who in Medicine, 1990.

- Outstanding Performance rating, 1989.

Certifications/Licenses/Accreditations

Certifications are written endorsements that you have met set standards or requirements through completion of a course of study and/or a written exam. Some occupations, such as education, medicine, and health require certification before you practice while in other occupational fields, such as finance and computers, certification is an enhancement.

Licenses are official documents that grant permission to perform activities or occupations. You'll need a license to operate a plane, car, or truck as well as practice law, social work, real estate, or perform notary public functions. Licenses also reflect seniority and compensation levels.

Accreditations certify individuals, often through proficiency exams, to fulfill official requirements.

Bar memberships should be organized in a separate section. Indicate the states where you passed bar exams.

You'll bolster your qualifications by including licensing and certification designations after your name. For example, frequently used acronyms include RN (Registered Nurse), CPA (Certified Public Accountant), CIA (Certified Internal Auditor), LCSW (Licensed Clinical Social Worker), and NCC (Nationally Certified Counselor).

Examples

- E1 Master Electrician, Commonwealth of Virginia

- Radon Measurement Operator-EPA Radon Proficiency Exam

- Maryland State Master Plumbing License, 1985

- ASMEL Commercial Pilot with instrument rating

- Licensed Private Single Engine Fixed Wing Pilot

- State Bar of Arizona

- California Real Estate License

- Certified Image Consultant, Color Me Beautiful

- Series 7 and 63 Brokerage Securities Licenses

- Certified New Home Sales Professional (CSP), 1995

- Registered Nurse—Commonwealth of Kentucky

- R.N.—Commonwealth of Virginia, Commonwealth of Pennsylvania (inactive), State of Ohio (inactive), State of California (inactive)

- American Heart Association: CPR, ACLS

- Registered Record Administrator (RRA)

- Notary Public

- Red Cross Certified First Aid, Red Cross Certified CPR, CPI (Crisis Prevention Intervention)

- X-Ray Certification, Monroe Community College, Rochester, New York, 1994

- Certified Food Service Manager, Queens County Health Department

- Standard Elementary Teaching Certificate, Elementary Grades, State of Oregon

- Virginia Post Graduate Professional Teacher Certificate Endorsements in Vocational Home Economics, Industrial Career Exploration, expires July 1, 2002

- Certified Reader for GED English Essay Examination

- State Medical Licenses; Virginia, Maryland, and District of Columbia

- Board Certified by National Commission on Certification of Physician Assistants, with recognition in primary care and surgery

- Firearms Training and Certification (re-certified bi-annually at Memphis Range), May 1987

- Registered Private Investigator, Commonwealth of Virginia, Department of Criminal Justice Services, active

Professional Affiliations

There are thousands of professional and trade associations and societies that represent every aspect of occupations, industries, and special interests. Membership in these organizations not only provides you with up-to-date information and resources to perform your job but also demonstrates to employers a commitment to your occupation. Leadership roles enhance your credentials even more.

List both the name of the organization and the acronym in parenthesis. Include any titles of leadership positions or committees. Do not include the designation member as it is assumed that you are a member.

As a rule of thumb, list only current affiliations. The exception would be organizations with prior membership where you performed key leadership roles or contributions.

Examples

- American Library Association, 1990-present

- Virginia Commission for the Arts, Regional Panelist, 1985-1990

- National Association of Purchasing Management, Purchasing Management

- Association of San Francisco, American Management Association

- Society of Automotive Engineers (SAE) and American Society of Mechanical Engineers (ASME)

- American Society for Training and Development (ASTD)

- American Counseling Association (ACA)

- American Association of Law Libraries
  President, 1995-present
  Executive Board Member, 1988-1990, 1994
  Executive Board Member, Private Law Libraries Special Interest Section, 1986-1987

- President and Member, Board of Trustees, The American Association of University Women

- The Sommelier Society of San Francisco, California
  Vice President, 1991, **Board of Directors**, 1991-present
  Designed and marketed a 10-week program for food and beverage
  professionals to increase their wine knowledge and generate sales.
  Achieved a 100% increase over previous enrollments. Recognized
  by Board of Directors for outstanding achievement.

Publications

Publications offer an excellent opportunity to demonstrate both written
communication skills and an expertise in your field. Consider including
any printed work that is offered for sale or distributed, including books,
articles, columns, theses, reports, papers, magazines, and newsletters.

State whether the work is published, unpublished, or when publication
in anticipated.

If your publications are extensive, consider separating them by type;
books, articles, and columns.

Use good judgement in selecting publications for inclusion. Articles
and books that have no relevance to the position you seek may take away
from your credentials.

Examples

- "Tall Tales," (a study of sexism in the elementary school), *American
  Journal of Education*, September 1995.

- Contributing Author, *Writers Guide to Publication*, American Writers
  Guild, Los Angeles, California, 1987

- Co-author and contributor to four functional activity guides, *Special
  Needs Strategies*, Stamford Special Education Center, Stamford,
  Connecticut, 1990-1994

- *Career Magic*, Career Press, Baltimore, Maryland, 1989

- "12-Step Approach to Resume Writing," *Ladies' Home Journal*,
  October 1995

- "Avoiding Math Anxiety in Female Teenagers," doctoral dissertation, Cornell University, Ithaca, New York, 1991

- "Computer Tips for Accountants," monthly column, *Professional Accountant Newsletter*, June 1994-August 1996

Extra, Extra

Identify any extra elements that make you a more desirable candidate. Are you willing to travel? Willing to relocate? These statements added at the end of your resume may enhance your candidacy.

Do you have security clearances? Determine how valuable this information is and format accordingly. If the clearance is highly desirable, include it in a separate section or centered at the end of your resume. You can include clearances that have expired if they bolster your credentials. Just state the level of clearance followed by inactive in parenthesis.

Have you been appointed or served on boards, commissions, or authorities? This can be included along with the honors section or organized as its own section.

Are you actively involved in your community? Membership, appointments, and participation in community, charitable, and civic organizations can be stated in a separate section titled Community Involvement.

7

Electronic Resumes

Resume distribution has come a long way. You'll find requests to "mail" your resume electronically in the newspaper employment classified sections and on homepages created by private and public sector organizations. The explosion of new technology enables you to bypass the post office, sending and storing your resume on a computer, via electronic mail (e-mail).

You'll need to prepare, organize, and format your resume differently to utilize options available through technology. As you conduct your employer research you'll identify if the employer prefers electronic resumes and or uses computer-based applicant tracking systems.

Resumes By E-mail

Forwarding your resume via e-mail may be the fastest and most appropriate way for you to respond to job openings; it can also produce a distorted resume if you don't carefully follow instructions.

In the world of leading technology, the process should be simple, but it isn't. Resumes are consistently delivered with wrap problems, skipped lines, and just overall illegible. The problem lies with the proliferation of word processing software and electronic mail programs, making it impossible to provide instructions that will work for every mix.

To make the most of this technology and avoid technical/appearance problems, follow closely any formatting instructions provided by employers.

Create a resume in ASCII (DOS text) to be forwarded via e-mail. Most word processing programs will generate letters in ASCII text and an ASCII version ensures an employer won't need to decipher or convert your resume to read it. Electronic resume text needs proper spacing as it will be read by both human and computer eyes.

Avoid encoded messages that compress the text to make the file smaller, transporting it quickly. Some electronic mail programs cannot handle encoded messages and the potential employer may receive your message quickly, but the text will be garbage.

Tips to Create an ASCII Resume

1. Open your word processing software and retrieve or open your resume file. Select "Save As" under the pull down file menu. There should be a location where you can select the file type "save as text file." Choose text with line breaks, ASCII Text (DOS), MS DOS Text, or ASCII Text (check your user manual for specific directions applicable to your word processing software). Change it to a text file with the file extension .txt.

2. Use a plain 7-bit ASCII text.

3. Upload the file and begin editing.

4. Most directions advise you to set your margins at 0 and 65. This didn't work with my word processing program; I was able to accomplish the same results by setting the right margin at 6.5 inches. This is crucial as it avoids wrapping your lines prematurely.

5. Use a fixed-width font, for example, 10 point Courier. Avoid proportional fonts that have different widths for different characters.

6. Don't use underlines, bold, and italic because ASCII is plain text and does not recognize formatting. If italics are necessary, use paired asterisks (*mm*) to symbolize italics.

7. Align all your text at the left. Don't use tabs; use line spacing to differentiate the different sections and paragraphs.

8. Choose a simple layout. Substitute graphics such as bullets with ASCII characters such as dashes (-) and asterisk (*).

9. Include street address, telephone and fax (if applicable) numbers, and electronic mail address.

10. Many electronic mail programs are pre-set to receive mail with a designated font. Even if you forward it in Courier and it is received in Arial, it should still transport closely to the format sent.

Ready, Set, Mail

1. Highlight all the resume text in your word processing document and copy it. Resumes that are copied and pasted tend to arrive more legible than resumes sent as an attachment.

2. Open your electronic mail program, open compose mail, and paste your copied resume in the file section.

3. Avoid sending resumes as attachments. Resume attachments are often illegible and some recruiters will forward your resume directly to their scanning system which may be unable to access attachments.

4. Use the subject section to indicate you're a job candidate. For example, "Programmer Candidate," "Resume Submission, "Skilled Programmer," or "Programmer Advertisement 1234" are just a few examples.

5. Print out your message before forwarding. There may be some shift in text and spacing while transferring the document from word

processing to your electronic mail program.

6. Correct any spacing problems. Make sure the left margins are all in line.

7. It's easy to make a mistake when typing in the address. Check it prior to sending your e-mail.

8. Always conduct a test to make sure your resume arrives clear. Send an e-mail copy to a friend or colleague.

9. Don't use page numbers on your electronic resume. You can't be sure where the page breaks will be and your name and page numbers in the wrong place just clutter the text.

10. Remember to make this just a text document. Special tools used in word processing programs don't work here, for example, using the control and enter keys for a page break. These techniques will scramble your text and you'll wind up sending an unreadable document.

Electronic Resume Samples

What follows is an electronic resume sample, as it looks when copied and pasted in an electronic mail program. The second sample demonstrates how the same resume looked when delivered to an employer's electronic mail system.

ROBERT L. DRYDEN
8712 Palm Drive
Culver City, California 90224
Work (310) XXX-XXXX
Home (310) XXX-XXXX

SUMMARY

Experienced programmer analyst with expertise in COBOL, JCL, MVS, VSAM, CICS, and DB2 software applications.

Progressive background in software design/development, structured analysis and design techniques, software development life cycle, software development methodology, information engineering, CASE tools, process modeling, data modeling, quality assurance, and software evaluation.

Trained in Visual Basic, experienced with client server applications, and strong interest in working with two and three tier application systems.

COMPUTER SKILLS

COBOL II, FoxBase, SqlBase by Gupta, DB2, CICS, Lotus Notes, TSO/SPF, Clist, OS/MVS/XA, Image/View, Assembler, Novell Netware, Application Development System (ADS), Lotus 1-2-3, Easy Flow, WordPerfect.

EXPERIENCE

PROGRAMMER/ANALYST
Pacific Coast Credit Union, Los Angeles, California, 1993 - present

Participate in a business re-engineering effort utilizing CASE tools and Yourdon methodology; gather requirements using JAD sessions.

Write functional specifications for Mortgage and a Member Record image/work flow systems including reports, definition of queues, file updates, definition of maturation dates for documents on DASD, optical, and shelf life, and new screen developments. Define document forms, tabs, folder layouts, and collection types.

Communicate effectively with department heads and key staff members to identify individual department needs/requirements. Program system to generate reports to satisfy needs.

Implemented and customized a purchased subsystem, VSR, which inserted electronic coded documents into the Image Plus database. Gathered additional requirements for new reports; maintained and enhanced the current systems. Utilized JCL, COBOL II, CICS, and DB2 in programming efforts.

Conceived and implemented method to produce customized access to organize reporting requirements by department.

PROGRAMMER/ANALYST
Technical Support Services, Los Angeles, California, 1990 - 1993

Enhanced and maintained a COBOL- and VSAM-based payroll system. Prepared files, created reports, and modified existing code as requested by oil company officials. This system processed worldwide employees wages for Union Oil Company.

LEADER/SENIOR SYSTEMS ANALYST
Federal Support Inc.(FSI), Washington, D.C., 1988 - 1990

Supported a contract for Federal Emergency Management Agency (FEMA). Installed, maintained, developed, and trained in support of a FoxBase audit system, HelpLAN. Gathered client requirements and wrote detail specifications. The system tracked the accomplishments of the U.S. Corp of Engineers along with the expenditures incurred for the disaster superfund.

Served as site leader for two offices within the General Service Administration (GSA). Scheduled production, maintained and developed the existing systems, established a new system using a client server DBMS (SQLBase), and downsized a COBOL system into a SQLBase system. Assigned work to team members, provided quality assurance, scheduled and tracked all assignments, provided status and financial reports, recommended new hires, and directed communications between GSA and FSI staffs.

Successfully delivered diverse projects on time. Wrote benchmark and prototype specifications, evaluated and recommended a client server DBMS; developed and implemented an audit sub-system; wrote general and detail design documents.

PROGRAMMER ANALYST
The Computer Company, Los Angeles, California, 1986 - 1988

Developed a reutilization system on Convergent Technology hardware (alias the

C-3 NGEN) employing an ADS data base for the Pentagon's excess automatic data processing equipment, EEIS. The reutilization system was successfully implemented and now operates in an on-line production environment. The EEIS developmental project was completed.

Headed a project to re-design the ADPE data system onto client server platform.

PROGRAMMER ANALYST
Sun Insurance Company, San Diego, California, 1983 - 1985

Maintained and enhanced an Accounting, Budget and Cost (ABC) system, a major financial system containing approximately 60 different jobs.

Aided development of a sub system, referred to as the Cost Allocation System (CAS), developed in order to produce Profit and Loss Statements and other accounting reports.

EDUCATION

San Diego Mesa College, San Diego, California
Master level courses in Information Systems

University of California, Los Angeles, Los Angeles, California Certificate, Post Graduate Studies in Information Systems, 1982
Bachelor of Science, Administrative and Management, 1980

Robinson, Wade @ RES

From:	SHResumes
To:	Robinsow
Subject:	Programmer position #6666
Date:	Tuesday, October 22, 1996 9:38AM

ROBERT L. DRYDEN
8712 Palm Drive
Culver City, California 90224
Work (310) XXX-XXXX
Home (310) XXX-XXXX

SUMMARY

Experienced programmer analyst with expertise in COBOL, JCL, MVS, VSAM, CICS, and DB2 software applications.

Progressive background in software design/development, structured analysis and design techniques, software development life cycle, software development methodology, information engineering, CASE tools, process modeling, data modeling, quality assurance, and software evaluation.

Trained in Visual Basic, experienced with client server applications, and strong interest in working with two and three tier application systems.

COMPUTER SKILLS

COBOL II, FoxBase, SqlBase by Gupta, DB2, CICS, Lotus Notes, TSO/SPF, Clist, OS/MVS/XA, Image/View, Assembler, Novell Netware, Application Development System (ADS), Lotus 1-2-3, Easy Flow, WordPerfect.

EXPERIENCE

PROGRAMMER/ANALYST
Pacific Coast Credit Union, Los Angeles, California, 1993 - present

Participate in a business re-engineering effort utilizing CASE tools and Yourdon methodology; gather requirements using JAD sessions.

Write functional specifications for Mortgage and a Member Record image/work flow systems including reports, definition of queues, file updates, definition of maturation dates for documents on DASD, optical, and shelf life, and new screen developments. Define document forms, tabs, folder layouts, and collection types.

Communicate effectively with department heads and key staff members to identify individual department needs/requirements. Program system to generate reports to satisfy needs.

Implemented and customized a purchased subsystem, VSR, which inserted electronic coded documents into the Image Plus database. Gathered additional requirements for new reports; maintained and enhanced the current systems. Utilized JCL, COBOL II, CICS, and DB2 in programming efforts.

Conceived and implemented method to produce customized access to organize reporting requirements by department.

PROGRAMMER/ANALYST
Technical Support Services, Los Angeles, California, 1990 - 1993

Enhanced and maintained a COBOL- and VSAM-based payroll system. Prepared files, created reports, and modified existing code as requested by oil company officials. This system processed worldwide employees wages for Union Oil Company.

LEADER/SENIOR SYSTEMS ANALYST
Federal Support Inc.(FSI), Washington, D.C., 1988 - 1990

Supported a contract for Federal Emergency Management Agency (FEMA). Installed, maintained, developed, and trained in support of a FoxBase audit system, HelpLAN. Gathered client requirements and wrote detail specifications. The system tracked the accomplishments of the U.S. Corp of Engineers along with the expenditures incurred for the disaster superfund.

Served as site leader for two offices within the General Service Administration (GSA). Scheduled production, maintained and developed the existing systems, established a new system using a client server DBMS (SQLBase), and downsized a COBOL system into a SQLBase system. Assigned work to team members, provided quality assurance, scheduled and tracked all assignments, provided status and financial reports, recommended new hires, and directed communications between GSA and FSI staffs.

Successfully delivered diverse projects on time. Wrote benchmark and prototype specifications, evaluated and recommended a client server DBMS; developed and implemented an audit sub-system; wrote general and detail design documents.

PROGRAMMER ANALYST
The Computer Company, Los Angeles, California, 1986 - 1988

Developed a reutilization system on Convergent Technology hardware (alias the C-3 NGEN) employing an ADS data base for the Pentagon's excess automatic data processing equipment, EEIS. The reutilization system was successfully implemented and now operates in an on-line production environment. The EEIS developmental project was completed.

Headed a project to re-design the ADPE data system onto client server platform.

PROGRAMMER ANALYST
Sun Insurance Company, San Diego, California, 1983 - 1985

Maintained and enhanced an Accounting, Budget and Cost (ABC) system, a major financial system containing approximately 60 different jobs.

Aided development of a sub system, referred to as the Cost Allocation System (CAS), developed in order to produce Profit and Loss Statements and other accounting reports.

EDUCATION

San Diego Mesa College, San Diego, California
Master level courses in Information Systems

University of California, Los Angeles, Los Angeles, California Certificate,
Post Graduate Studies in Information Systems, 1982
Bachelor of Science, Administrative and Management, 1980

8

Scannable Resumes

Organizational downsizing has increased the number of resumes in circulation while it's decreased the number of staff members to review them. Computer-based applicant tracking systems solve the problem for organizations that have been inundated with resumes, are unable to manage the flow, and are taking too long to manually review them.

Computer-based applicant tracking systems easily handle and scan large volumes of resumes. Some organizations are using them exclusively, eliminating manual processing and paper storage entirely. The systems quickly identify, sort, and store individual's credentials and recognize those most qualified for open positions. Systems can be customized to meet user (employer) needs and enable users to set up the criteria for each job opening, extract key qualification information, assign weights based on a sliding scale to the level of importance for qualifications, and automatically match the most qualified candidates with open positions.

The majority of resumes received for scanning arrive through the mail. Some systems allow you to fax or e-mail your resume directly into the system. Many organizations keep your resume active in their databases for periods ranging from 6 to 12 months.

Systems with artificial intelligence can extract information and scan for skills (key words). Computer-based applicant tracking systems are projected to decline in price, making them available to more employers, regardless of organizational size. The scanning devices enable employers to track, view, print, store, and acknowledge resumes. Human resources professionals and staffing specialists predict that automated resume systems may lead to a paperless workplace, minimizing filing and resume loss.

Once resumes are scanned into a computer system, Optical Character Recognition (OCR) software reads and identifies every letter, number, and mark it can find. The computer creates a text file (ASCII) of all the information it's been able to identify and organize. The most sophisticated systems will store three copies of your resume: the original scanned image, the OCR'd text, and an extracted summary.

Computer-based applicant tracking systems are set to search for key words that make up job requirements or requisition criteria. The system will search the database and identify the strongest matches for the job specifications. The more key words in your resume that match requirements (known as "hits"), the more likely your resume will make the preferred candidate list, the most qualified applicants ranked in order of qualifications.

Some organizations seeking employees in specific geographical areas may use area codes and zip codes as key words.

Should You Create a Scannable Resume?

When doing your employer research, determine whether or not an organization of interest scans resumes. Check to see if an organization has a homepage and if they offer application or scannable resume guidelines online or through their employment office. More and more employment classified advertisements indicate whether the organization scans resumes.

It's critical to follow employer application instructions if you are to be considered for employment. Each employer is different and has their own guidelines: whether in the organization of your information, the maximum number of pages, the inclusion of your social security number, font type, size, and special effects.

A recent employment classified advertisement carried the following instructions:

"For consideration you must reference the department number. Please adhere to these guidelines to ensure scannability—white paper, standard fonts (i.e. Courier or Helvetica), minimum 10 point type, do not use bold, italics, underlines, fancy fonts, boxes, graphics, or borders." Included was a standardized choice of response "three avenues—e-mail, fax and snail mail."

You can also telephone hiring managers or human resources departments and inquire "Are you using a computer-based applicant tracking system or resume scanning system?" and if they give an affirmative answer, it will be helpful to find out which one. Computer-based applicant tracking system manufacturers, such as Resumix, offer their own guidelines for preparing ideal scannable resumes. You can check directly with manufacturers or access their homepages to determine their instructions.

Career changers have traditionally showcased their transferrable skills in a functional format. Computer-based applicant tracking systems will make it more difficult for individuals to use this method to attract employer attention.

Key Words

Key words, also known as buzzwords, are technical, industry, or skill terms (often nouns but also adjectives and adverbs) that indicate your skills, abilities, experience, education, professional licenses, certifications, and affiliations. These key words should be common in your occupation and industry. The more key words you include, the greater the odds that your resume will be selected from a computer-based applicant tracking system.

Key words are so important in scannable resumes that many individuals include a key word summary that includes their job titles, areas of experience, and skills. The key word summary can either precede or replace a qualifications summary.

Avoid redundant use of key words; there is usually no increase in ranking if multiple key words are utilized. Creatively use statements and synonyms, for example, include "dBase, Paradox, and FoxPro" in one section and "three years of experience with PC-based relational databases" in another section. Or, "Fluent in foreign languages" in one section and "Fluent in German and French, conversant in Spanish" in another section.

Be specific in detailing your qualifications. A scanning system searching for the keyword Lotus 1-2-3 will make a "hit" or match if you've taken a course, even if you have no practical experience. The "hit" or match can put you in the running if your other credentials balance out or outweigh other job seekers. In another example, a job seeker who has extensive benefits experience applies for a benefits/compensation specialist position. She has no practical compensation experience but details in her resume two courses in compensation management. This training scores a "hit" and may make her a desirable candidate despite the lack of practical experience.

Maximize "hits" by including all of your skills in specific terms. It is too generic to indicate experience with IBM operating systems, instead state MVS. Substitute Oracle or Sybase for client server databases. Elaborate on "Teach seventh and eighth grade" to "Teach Civics to seventh and eighth grade students with a specialty in the establishment and implementation of a model Congress program."

There is no industry standard for job requirements and each organization may select different criteria for their positions. You'll need to identify and develop a list of key words and qualifications you feel will meet most organizational requirements.

Tips to Generate Key Words

1. Utilize your networking contacts to locate copies of job descriptions.

2. The newspaper classified employment advertisements are an easy and accessible resource to identify job requirements.

3. Join professional associations and build your list from descriptions, lists of accomplishments and achievements, and articles found in journals and newsletters.

4. Contact association members and leaders to identify occupational and industry requirements.

5. Access the homepages of different organizations (particularly any of interest) to locate descriptions, skills, and desirable qualifications.

6. Use informational interviewing, both in person and telephone, to request professional, educational, and personal qualifications for the jobs you seek.

7. Request and read literature from organizations of interest to identify

the organizational culture, personality, and mission. The statements may include descriptive words (key words) the organization prefers in job candidates.

8. Review occupational handbooks, bulletins, journals, and studies produced by the U.S. Department of Labor, Bureau of Labor Statistics.

9. Research occupational literature, both hard copy and online. You'll find books and periodicals dedicated to occupations and college majors.

10. Look for mentoring programs sponsored by academic, government, community, social service, and non-profit organizations. Mentors in your career field are a wonderful source of occupational and industry information.

Resume Differences and Similarities

All resumes must be clear and professional, making it easy for the human and computer eyes to read.

Differences

1. A scannable resume is usually longer than a traditional resume. Traditional resumes are one to two pages in length while scannable resumes can be three or more pages. Include your entire work history to ensure that all of your skills are highlighted and described to meet job requirements, unless the application or scannable resume guidelines tell you differently.

2. Scannable resumes go back further and are more comprehensive than traditional resumes.

3. Experiences and skills must be elaborated as the computer system, no matter how sophisticated, does not assume that because you have one skill, you have subskills that usually make up that skill. For example, if you state "administer nursing care," the system will

not presume that you "perform nursing care in acute care, post-op, and emergency settings including IVS, medications, blood pressures, and patient and family training." You will need to elaborate on all your skills and experience.

4. Maximize key word "hits" with jargon, the technical and specialized vocabulary used by members of your particular profession.

5. While automated scanning systems seem to be biased and work most favorably towards high-tech jobs, these systems will be used more and more to scan for all types of openings.

6. Recent college graduates need to depend on internships, externships, volunteer experience, practicums, simulations, course work, and academic involvement to meet qualifications and requirements.

7. Professional training, even in lieu of practical experience, will count towards meeting qualifications.

8. Simplicity is the key for scannable resumes. Scanning equipment reads text and not graphics.

Similarities

1. Center your name on the first page of the resume. Follow with your complete mailing address and phone numbers.

2. Place your name on the succeeding pages of the resume with page number.

3. Avoid abbreviations, with an exception of college degrees.

4. Balance the resume with plenty of white space. Use a one inch margin on both sides, top, and bottom.

5. Produce the cleanest copies with a laser or ink jet printer. Avoid dot matrix. Send originals or high quality photocopies.

6. Print or photocopy resumes on 8 ½- by 11-inch quality paper, white

or light-colored (cream, beige, or buff). Avoid mottled or marbled papers and dark colors.

7. Use standard typefaces. Choose from Arial, Times Roman, Century Schoolbook, Helvetica, Optima, and Palatino. The best font sizes are 10 to 14 point. Don't use Times Roman in 10 point; it's hard for the computer and human eye to read.

8. Avoid newspaper-style columns or tabular arrangements.

10 Tips to Prepare Scannable Resumes

1. If you know your resume will be scanned with an automated resume system, use only a chronological format. Use left justification for the entire document.

2. Write descriptive sentences. Follow the same suggestions provided in the experience chapter.

3. Continue to use action verbs but enhance your descriptions by selecting nouns and adjectives. This combination serves three purposes: it will catch the reader's eye, illustrate your experience, and provide key words for the scanning device. You'll be surprised to learn that computers will be searching for nouns in college names such as Harvard, Stanford, or Yale (and can differentiate between Harvard University, 88 Harvard Street, and the software program Harvard Graphics) and organizational names like IBM, Deloitte Touche, or The New York Times.

4. Summaries play an integral part in all resumes. Qualifications and special skill and experience areas are featured and the text captures key words for the scanning device. Increase the likelihood of a match with a key word summary.

5. Industry and occupational acronyms and jargon are not only acceptable, they are favorable. Scanning devices may be set to search for key words that are standard acronyms and you'll miss a match if they're not stated. Make sure you spell out acronyms that

are not an industry standard or used only in your organization and initially spell common place acronyms.

6. Include as many skills and facts as you can; the more information listed, the greater potential of a match. If you are stating technical terms, describe them in the most generic or standard way to match the job requirements.

7. Italic, script, and underlining features don't scan well. Uppercase scans well so use this feature to balance and indicate the importance of items on your scannable resume.

8. Save the bullets, ruling lines, boxes, and special desktop publishing features for traditional resumes; these features don't scan well.

9. Some organizations do not even want bold. Before using bold text, check for application requirements to see if it is acceptable. When in doubt, do without bold.

10. Do not fold or staple the resume. Mail in a 9- by 12-inch envelope.

9

Answers Please

The prior chapters detailed all the elements you need to write and pull together a winning resume. You may still have a few questions that apply to your particular circumstances or you may need answers to specific problems or questions.

I've asked job seekers just like you for the most complex, difficult, and confusing questions on resume writing. Read through this chapter and you'll find ideas, suggestions, and directions that answer some of the trickiest and most troublesome resume questions.

Question: Someone asked me to send them my vitae. What is a vitae and do I use that as well as a resume?

Answer: A vitae (usually identified as a curriculum vitae) is an autobiographical sketch frequently used by academic and medical professionals. It is usually longer than a resume and includes education, experience, publications, presentations, continuing education, licenses, and board certifications. If you were to use a vitae you would use it in place of a resume.

Question: I'm having trouble getting started with my resume. What should my focus be?

Answer: Make it easy for employers to see your qualifications and reach you. Use a straightforward format, avoid cluttering the resume with information that has no relevance to the jobs you seek, include all details that demonstrate that you meet job requirements, and be accessible by indicating telephone, e-mail, pager, or fax numbers.

Question: What do you mean make it easy for employers to see my qualifications?

Answer: Tailor your resume to meet employer needs/requirements. Identify what education, training, experience, skills, certifications/licenses are required for the position(s) you seek. Match your credentials and focus the content and format of your resume to demonstrate that you meet the requirements.

Question: Should I use my work phone number? If I do, won't it appear that I'm looking for a job during my work hours?

Answer: I would advise against looking for a job during your work hours but, I feel that it is fine to use a work phone number. It is essential that prospective employers reach you and I would give them all the phone numbers that will enable them to do just that. You can always take the message and return the call during your lunch hour or before/after working hours.

Question: What's the best way to produce a resume?

Answer: Resumes should be produced so they can be stored and are easy to modify and update as you move through the job search process. Choose word processing or resume software programs, word processors, or desktop publishing software. All of these sources will enable you to make changes in content and format.

Question: I read that you don't include high school on your resume and yet I have no education beyond high school. What do I do?

Answer: Did you attend a vocational, trade, apprenticeship, or professional school/program? Have you taken any training, courses, or workshops since high school? Any of these can be included under an education, professional development, or a training section and you can eliminate high school. If you have none of these, include high school and make a commitment to get some training in your field to replace high school in the education section.

Question: Should I include military experience?

Answer: There is no firm rule whether you should include or exclude your military experience. Will it weaken or overload your experience? Can you translate the experience so it is both relevant and applicable to the industry or sector you're seeking to enter? Some job seekers feel it adds to their credentials and others take great pride in their service and want to include it. If you choose to include it, either integrate it into your experience chronology or, follow with a separate section titled Military Experience.

Question: I'd like to use a post office box number on my resume rather than a street address. If I do, will employers think I'm unstable?

Answer: Use a post office box number if you are in transition, moving from one location to another, and have no current fixed address. A post office box will make you accessible to employers while enabling you to retrieve your mail. This is the only appropriate reason to use a post office box rather than a street address.

Question: Can I include volunteer experience?

Answer: Experience is experience whether it is paid or unpaid. Determine whether the unpaid experience is relevant to the jobs you seek, enhances or strengthens your credentials, or makes you a more qualified candidate. If so, include it. Career changers have effectively used unpaid experience to develop skills, experience, and contacts to transition into a new career or industry.

Question: I have extensive publications. Do I include them all?

Answer: Publications are a credential and demonstrate an expertise in your field of interest. Beware of including any publications that are not related to the position you seek. If all the publications are relevant to the position and you are afraid the list is overwhelming, select the most recent and/or those from the most recognized publications.

Question: If an employer indicates I can mail or fax my resume, which one should I choose?

Answer: Do both. Fax your resume first along with a cover letter and follow up with a hard copy through the mail.

Question: If I have the choice to mail, fax, or e-mail my resume, which one is preferable?

Answer: I would choose to e-mail your resume using ASCII text, making sure to include your own e-mail number.

Question: If the employment classified advertisements or the organizational application requirements don't indicate whether the organization accepts or prefers faxed resumes, do I inquire whether to fax anyway?

Answer: Adhere to stated preferences, whether in the advertisement or application guidelines, as some computer-based applicant tracking systems cannot scan faxed resumes; if an organization of interest uses one of these systems, a faxed resume might put you out of the running.

Question: If I fax my resume, do I need a cover sheet and a cover letter?

Answer: You need to fax a cover letter and if you are using a cover letter and it is directed properly, you don't need a cover sheet. Once again, check employer preferences. I recently read an employment classified advertisement where the employer stated not to send a cover letter but use a cover sheet.

Question: If an organization uses a scanning system for my resume, will my cover letter be scanned too?

Answer: Some organizations will scan your cover letter. Cover letters often include details more specific to the job opportunity (such as geographical preference) and may generate additional "hits."

Question: Some faxes send poor copies. How can I make sure mine arrives as professional and clear as possible?

Answer: When using a stand alone fax machine, use an original or a quality copy of your resume and cover letter. Set the fax mode to "fine mode" (fax machines and fax boards) to ensure your recipient receives the best quality copy.

Question: Do I need to follow up all faxed resumes and cover letters with hard copies?

Answer: Yes, you should. Tailor your cover letter by changing your first line to read, "This letter and resume are copies of originals faxed to your attention on May 13, 19XX" or "This is a follow-up copy to my resume and letter faxed on May 13, 19XX."

Question: I've heard a lot about electronic resume databases. What are they?

Answer: Resume databases are available to store your resume, making your resume available 24 hours a day, accessible to employers all over the country who use the database. Some services are free while others charge annual memberships.

Question: This sounds too good to be true. What are the drawbacks?

Answer: There is no documented proof that this is a successful means of finding jobs. Only 10% to 15% of all jobs are found through employment classified advertisements and while there have been no studies done, you would probably find much less of a percentage with this form than the classifieds.

Question: What are the possibilities of someone copying my resume?

Answer: That is a real risk when placing your resume in an electronic job bank that is accessible to anyone. Other job seekers can download your resume and use it as a guide or model to produce their own. On the flip side, you can search for resumes from job seekers with similar work experience to learn how they have presented their qualifications.

Question: I'm confused about sending an electronic resume. I'd really just like to send my resume as an attachment.

Answer: Be careful of what and how you send information electronically. If an employer finds the message "Too large to fit in memory" and/or lots of blank space and junk, it will probably knock you out of the running.

Question: Should I set up my own homepage for my resume and e-mail employers with that information so they can access my homepage?

Answer: Many employers, large and small, use e-mail systems that are on their LANs, in other words, office environments are on their own networks. They can respond to your e-mail but have to set up an alias in their mail system to send a separate message (for example, accessing your homepage).

Question: Should I use a resume software program to prepare my resume?

Answer: Resume software programs often have limits with spacing, fonts and sizes, and the number of characters on a line. I prefer the flexibility word processing and desktop publishing gives, enabling the user to format information in the way they find most effective and flattering. If you want to use a resume software program, make sure you will be able to adapt the style sheets to fit your needs.

Question: What is a style sheet?

Answer: Style sheets (also known as templates) are used in desktop publishing, word processing, and resume software programs to format documents. They are computer files that control the text attributes (such as font and line spacing), margins, paragraphs, indentations, headings, and special effects.

Question: What are human resources professionals looking for when they evaluate a resume?

Answer: Organizations have positions to fill and anyone screening your resume wants to know that you have the qualifications to fill an open position. Resumes must demonstrate that you meet job requirements.

Question: But what if I don't match the job qualifications 100%. Should I apply anyway, and if so, how do I word my resume to make up for the lack of some of the required skills?

Answer: Yes, you should apply even if there isn't a 100% match. Indicate in your cover letter that while you don't have all the necessary qualifications, you do meet specific requirements, and identify those. Use your letter to demonstrate how you can make a contribution.

Question: Should I send more than one copy of my resume?

Answer: As a rule you should send only one. If you speak with a hiring manager and they are unable to locate your resume, you can send them a copy.

Question: How do I explain the years I stayed home when my children were small?

Answer: What did you do on a professional level during those years? Did you participate in professional organizations, conduct fundraising campaigns, organize large-scale meetings? What seminars, workshops, or courses did you attend? Did you consult, learn a marketable skill, or write a newsletter? These are the types of experiences that help fill gaps in employment. If you have none of them, consider participating while you prepare your resume and plan your job search. If not, you will have gaps and will need to explain in an interview that you took time off to raise your family.

Question: How do I decide how many years of employment to show? I am concerned about age discrimination?

Answer: Each case is different and needs to be evaluated individually. Is there an experience way back in your history that relates to the position under consideration? Do you feel indicating the last 12 years or 3 employers is enough? You need to determine once again what qualifications demonstrate that you meet job requirements and include those. Remember that your resume is not set in stone. Make adjustments and modifications to your resume as you work through your job search.

Question: As a career changer I prefer to use a functional resume. Is a functional resume difficult to scan?

Answer: Yes it is. Every application requirement I have seen for computer-based applicant tracking systems indicates they want chronological resumes. Career changers that use functional resumes need to pursue opportunities with companies that do not use scanning systems and through networking and personal contact.

Question: I have done a lot of volunteer work with my church and I belong to a number of religious organizations. Can I include this in my resume?

Answer: Are you applying for a job that is related to your religion or within your church community? If you are, those are the only circumstances that would merit inclusion. I always encourage individuals to prepare resumes that omit any information that reflects religion, color, race, sex, or national origin.

Question: I am confused about career objectives. How do I know if I should use one or a summary or can I use both?

Answer: Summaries are not required but they are a wonderful introduction for your experience and talents. It's an effective way to capture an employer's attention. If you have a specific career objective you certainly can use it. I like using career objectives with summaries but if you are a recent college graduate or have little work experience, a career objective by itself may be most appropriate.

Question: Should I somehow mention in my resume that my present employer is unaware that I am looking for another job and I want to keep my job search confidential?

Answer: our cover letter is the appropriate place to mention this information. State your request for confidentiality in your last paragraph, for example, "While I have enjoyed my tenure with ABC company, my current position no longer offers me the challenge I seek. I would appreciate your confidentiality in my current job search."

Question: I don't want to do my resume myself. How do I find someone to prepare my resume?

Answer: Begin your search by asking friends and colleagues to recommend a service or an individual they have used. Locate resume services in the telephone business directories. Ask questions concerning the individual's experience, track record, and process. Cost is important and should fit your budget, but the preparer's qualifications should weigh more heavily in your decision. Look for services that provide personal attention to preparing resumes that demonstrate that you meet job requirements.

10

Resume Samples

The following resumes illustrate how you can transform the tips, techniques, suggestions, sentences, and paragraphs from the previous chapters into a powerful and job-getting resume.

Read through all the resumes and you'll become a pro in presenting your qualifications. Focus on how accomplishments, experience, skills, publications, and credentials are featured. Learn how to bolster education without a college degree and downplay incomplete education, short work history, and gaps in employment. See first-hand how to finesse a career change, integrate consulting and diverse experiences, and use chronological and functional type formats to your advantage.

Seeing is believing and you'll quickly master how to convert traditional resumes into scannable and electronic resumes. Check out the **programmer** example, a traditional resume, on page 131. What follows is the same resume transformed into a scannable resume on page 133 and an electronic resume on page 135. Another conversion takes place for a **teacher** example, a traditional resume, on page 146, re-worked into a scannable resume on page 147.

Below is an index of resumes by occupation. You'll also find a key to easily locate the functional, chronological, scannable, and electronic examples.

Resumes By Occupation

Resumes By Types and Formats

MICHAEL SILVER, CIA
85 Coastline Drive
Ontario, California 91760
(714) XXX-XXXX

CAREER SUMMARY

Innovative, experienced auditor with an expertise in identifying opportunities to utilize technology, increasing audit department efficiency and effectiveness.

PROFESSIONAL EXPERIENCE

ORANGE COUNTY, 1981 - present

Audit Manager, 1987 - present

Plan and supervise audit projects and develop long range audit plans for the Internal Audit Office. Manage all phases for projects in progress for two audit teams. Review progress ensuring audits are completed on time and within budget. Edit and revise draft reports. Train audit staff in the use of personal computers.

- Recommended opportunities for personal computer use. Oversaw selection and installation of personal computers throughout internal audit department. Appointed to Microcomputer Management Committee.

- Managed audit projects resulting in estimated savings or cost avoidance opportunities of over $2.8 million since 1991.

- Initiated, developed, and implemented a Software Compliance Action Plan for Orange County, minimizing the County's exposure to litigation from software vendors for copyright infringement.

- Selected to serve as one of five members of Orange County Privatization Action Team responsible for overseeing privatization of County services. Initial projects included vehicle and facilities maintenance and child care for school age children. Conceived and developed a cost allocation plan for allocating costs of general government administration to programs identified for privatization. Participated in contract negotiations with vendors.

Senior Auditor, 1981 - 1987

Conducted major projects as auditor in charge. Planned and conducted financial, compliance, and operational audits for County agencies and non-profit organizations. Monitored compliance with California State Code for non-profit organizations conducting bingo games and raffles. Designed and implemented a departmental reporting system for tracking County payments from real estate developers.

- Created a *Bingo Accounting Guide*, adopted for use statewide.

MICHAEL SILVER   PAGE 2

SAN MATEO COUNTY, 1979 - 1981

Staff Auditor, 1979 - 1981

Conducted financial and compliance audits of County departments. Audited Federal Department of Labor grants under the Comprehensive Employment and Training Act (CETA).

INSTITUTE OF INTERNAL AUDITORS, 1982 - present

The Auditor
  Contributing Editor, 1989 - 1994

Established a column, "Computers and Auditing," reporting methods for auditors to use microcomputers and achieve audit and administrative objectives. Reviewed soft-ware applications beneficial to internal auditors. Wrote column; edited manuscripts from contributors.

International Committees
  Member of Editorial Advisory Board, 1989 - present
  Membership Committee, 1986 - 1989

Orange County Chapter
  Member, Board of Governors, 1990 - present
  Chapter President, 1988-1989. Chapter received the "Gold Award" in the Chapter Achievement Program for the first time.
  Past Vice President Professional Development, 1987
  Past Membership Chair, 1985

TRAINING AND PRESENTATION EXPERIENCE

Teach numerous workshops in Accounting and Internal Auditing at the Graduate School, U.S. Department of Agriculture Government Audit Training Institute and Orange County Adult and Community Education, 1984 - present

Create and present workshops to professional audit associations, local colleges, and universities.

CERTIFICATION

Certified Internal Auditor (CIA), 1982

EDUCATION

M.S., Accounting, University of California, Irvine, Irvine, California, 1979
B.A., Economics, Pepperdine University, Malibu, California, 1970

TRICIA G. RICHARDSON
88 Mission Square, San Francisco, California 94110
(415) XXX-XXXX

CAREER SUMMARY

Highly skilled food service manager with excellent culinary skills. Extensive experience in fine dining restaurants, luxury hotels, conference centers, and institutional operations.

Experienced manager and trainer with exceptional organization and problem-solving skills. Ability to work well with all staff from line to executive level.

EXPERIENCE

EXECUTIVE SOUS CHEF
The Madison Hotel, San Francisco, California, 1989 - 1997

Managed food service operation and staff of 20 for a 236-room luxury property with combined banquet facilities for 800, 24-hour room service, fine dining restaurant, lounge, and employee cafeteria. Supervised stewarding department with staff of 15.

Created and standardized menu concepts. Effectively controlled costs and met sanitation requirements. Interviewed, hired, trained, scheduled, counseled, fired, and appraised performance; prepared payroll.

CHEF INSTRUCTOR
Army Military Personnel Command, Washington, D.C., 1986 - 1989

Evaluated operations and initiated changes and upgrades to food and beverage preparation, production, and service in U.S. Army Club System worldwide.

Trained and developed civilian and military food service personnel; customized and tailored training to meet individual staff and club needs. Assessed staffing, equipment, and inventory; developed long-range goals and directions for this international food service organization.

EXECUTIVE CHEF
Sammy's, Palo Alto, California, 1982 - 1985

Managed food services for elegant jazz supper club with a piano lounge, fine dining room, and banquet facilities for 200.

CHEF SAUCIER
The Wine Cellar, Sheraton Hotel (formerly The Bay Hotel), San Francisco, California, 1980 - 1982

Progressive promotions to positions of increased responsibility in a luxury hotel.

EDUCATION

CULINARY INSTITUTE OF AMERICA, Associate of Occupational Studies, Hyde Park, New York, 1980
Completed four-month externship at The Sonoma Inn and Country Club, Sonoma, California, an exclusive conference center and resort featuring private country club dining room, public fine dining room, and banquet facilities for 4,000.

UNIVERSITY OF KANSAS, Bachelor of Science, Culinary Science, Lawrence, Kansas, 1978

JOHN D. MYERS
8 Oakleaf Drive
Charleston, West Virginia 25300
(304) XXX-XXXX

CAREER OBJECTIVE

A position repairing or assembling equipment that requires a strong technical background and an ability to solve technical problems.

BACKGROUND SUMMARY

Qualified and experienced electrical technician with knowledge of electrical theory and advanced electronics theory. Expertise in electronics testing and repair.

- Highly skilled in reading circuit diagrams and assembling complex electrical components.
- Dependable and conscientious worker with excellent problem-solving skills, persevering to get the job done.

EXPERIENCE

Computer Technician, 1984-present
Computers Unlimited, Charleston, West Virginia

Quickly and efficiently test and repair personal computers and terminals at customer locations. Perform diagnostics, components repairs, and preventive maintenance. Promote customer satisfaction by sharing techniques for equipment operation and early problem identification.

Service Technician, 1976-1983
ABC Technologies, Charleston, West Virginia

Assembled, tested, and performed troubleshooting for a computer reseller. Involved in all processes, ensuring the equipment functioned properly. Developed a technical expertise and provided assistance to the repair department.

EDUCATION/TRAINING

Technical Institute, Wheeling, West Virginia
Completed courses in Basic Electronics, Introduction to Computer Systems, Central Processor Hardware and Software, and Peripheral Equipment

Wheeling Public Schools, Adult Education, Wheeling, West Virginia
Courses in Electronics, Radio and TV Repair

AMY R. MILLER
111 Fox Run Drive, Oakton, Virginia 22124
(703) XXX-XXXX   Fax (703) XXX-XXXX

Highly skilled career professional with extensive experience as a trainer, writer, and manager. Author of five career/job hunting books.

WORK HISTORY

MILLER & ASSOCIATES

Career Consultant, 1983 - present

- Own and operate a business specializing in job search support. Write and produce effective resumes and cover letters for individual clients. Provide customized resume writing services for multi-million dollar corporate proposals.

- Write speeches, marketing materials, books, and manuals; contribute articles to newsletters, magazines, and journals on job search and career planning/management topics.

- Develop, customize, and conduct speeches and training programs on job search and career development topics. Design curriculum; create and produce materials and workbooks. Frequent speaker and lecturer for corporate, academic, community, association, and governmental organizations. Appear as guest on radio talk shows and cable television.

FAIRFAX COUNTY ADULT EDUCATION

Career Planning Program Specialist, 1983 - 1992
Instructor, 1982 - 1992

- Administered career and life planning adult education program for the nation's tenth largest school district. Developed, coordinated courses; recruited, interviewed, hired, and supervised 25-30 instructors. Taught workshops in job search skills, career planning/changing, and professional development.

- Experienced 110% growth in student enrollment. Increased course offerings by 70%. Designed a career counseling program, developed alternative career work styles, entrepreneurship, career explorations, and job hunting preparation. Created programs with local high technology and health care industries, offering career exploration at the work site.

- Established and conducted outplacement workshops for Fairfax County Public Schools. Created and produced handbook, *Job Search Techniques*. Hired instructors and scheduled classes.

KATHARINE GIBBS SCHOOL

Instructor, 1986 - 1987

- Taught classes in "Introduction to Management," "Supervisory Management," "Effective Business Writing," and "Professionalism at Work."

XEROX CORPORATION

District Billing Manager, 1979 - 1980
Office Services Supervisor, 1978 - 1979
Customer Service Manager, 1974 - 1977
Administration, 1972 - 1974

- Managed staffs of 7 to 22; recruited, supervised, and developed position descriptions. Created and utilized training material. Established performance criteria and appraised performance.

- Successfully and consistently exceeded performance targets in billing and credit and collections.

AMY R. MILLER   PAGE 2

- Managed billing department for machine population of 16,000 units and annual revenue of $66 million. Developed and implemented credit and collection programs and maintained cash flows for $33 million in annual revenue.

- Administered a new major account price plan for 25 accounts; developed and presented a training program on complex contractual terms for senior-level customers, sales staff, and administrative personnel.

- Supervised administrative secretarial communication network for 22 secretaries supporting 200 managers. Established support position guides, performance standards, and secretarial handbooks. Conducted awareness seminars, team building workshops, and third party counseling.

EDUCATION

Bachelor of Arts in English, George Mason University, Fairfax, Virginia, 1981

Xerox Corporation Management Training: Management Studies, New Manager Seminar, Managing for Motivation, Management Action Workshop

PROFESSIONAL DEVELOPMENT

Strong Training Program, Qualifying Workshop, Consulting Psychologists Press (CPP), 1991

Myers-Briggs Type Indicator, Typewatching Qualifying Workshop, Otto Kroeger Associates, 1989

PUBLICATIONS

BOOKS

101 Resumes for Sure-Hire Results, AMACOM Books, New York, New York, 1994
Sure-Hire Cover Letters, AMACOM Books, New York, New York, 1994
The Whole Career Sourcebook, AMACOM Books, New York, New York, 1991
Sure-Hire Resumes, AMACOM Books, New York, New York, 1990
Resumes: The Write Stuff, Garrett Park Press, Garrett Park, Maryland, 1987

ARTICLES

"9 Tips On Using Excerpts To Sell Your Book," *Writer's Digest 1,082 Tips*, October 1995, *Writer's Digest*, January 1989
"Cover Letter Tips for Auditors," *Internal Auditing Alert*, July 1995
"Resume Writing Tips for Internal Auditors," *Internal Auditing Alert*, April 1995
"How To Use The Strong With High School Students," *User's Guide For the SVIB-SII*, Consulting Psychologists Press, 1994
"Person to Person," *Science and Engineering Horizons*, 1991/1992 Edition
"Push-Button Resumes," *Executive Female*, July/August 1990
"Writing a Great Cover Letter," *Image World*, May/June 1990
"1 Plan For Marketing Your Book To Libraries," *Writer's Digest*, December 1989
"Career Notes," monthly career column, *Sound Publications*, January 1988 - November 1989
"Resume Writing Tips and Traps," *IIA Today*, March/April 1989
"A 12-Step Approach To Career Success," *The Woman Engineer*, Fall 1988
"Resumes That Get Jobs," *Woman's Day*, March 1988

MARIA GOODHUE
NREMT-Paramedic

21 Rosetree Court   Home (804) XXX-XXXX
New Orleans, Louisiana 70115   Work (804) XXX-XXXX

QUALIFICATIONS SUMMARY

Solid experience and achievements in the field of emergency medical services. Bottom-line oriented administrator, efficiently managing staff and resources while consistently ensuring quality of care. Demonstrated ability to develop and maintain a team atmosphere while motivating staff to achieve operational objectives.

PROFESSIONAL EXPERIENCE

TULANE UNIVERSITY HOSPITAL, New Orleans, Louisiana, 1994-present
Manager, Emergency Life Support Education Center

♦ Direct the daily operations of a training center providing advanced and basic life support educational programs for 3,000 hospital employees, physicians, and medical students. Manage a staff of over 30 faculty members.

♦ As a Human Resources Division Head, participate in weekly human resources operational staff meetings.

♦ Oversee department billings and charges to the university and outside contracts.

♦ Contribute to quality of care as member of hospital code blue review and planning team.

♦ Restructured the department and saved 20% in overall budget without any reduction in quality of service.

♦ Instituted quality standards and increased department professionalism. Initiated and implemented department policies and procedures.

LACARE HEALTH SYSTEM, New Orleans, Louisiana, 1991-1994
Program Coordinator, Life Support Education

♦ Established and managed a program offering advanced and basic life support training to a two-state community. Implemented a local community education program. Instructed in BLS and ACLS.

♦ Successfully acquired approval by the American Heart Association and endorsement by the American College of Surgeons.

♦ Conducted environmental assessments, organized and marketed programs, hired staff, and obtained necessary resources.

♦ Cultivated relationships with professional staff and secured medical direction support.

♦ Oversaw training facility relocation and design to meet future medical training requirements.

♦ Co-authored a million dollar training contract to provide paramedic training to City of New Orleans Fire and Rescue Department.

Flight Paramedic, LACARE Medical Aircare

♦ Provided emergency and critical health care as member of medical flight team. Participated in marketing new medical flight service program and selecting emergency equipment to ensure optimal patient care.

MARIA GOODHUE   PAGE 2

ST. PETER HOSPITAL, Jackson, Mississippi, 1989-1991
Flight Paramedic, Jackson Life Flight

♦ Administered emergency and critical health care as member of medical flight team. Contributed to the hospital's implementation of a new approach to emergency care.

EMERGENCY MEDICAL SERVICES AUTHORITY (EMSA)/METRO AMBULANCE, Jackson, Mississippi, 1987-1989
Operations Manager/Paramedic

♦ Progressive promotions to a leadership role directing the daily operations of a public utility model EMS system responding to over 40,000 annual calls and serving a population of 300,000 covering approximately 1,000 square miles.

MEMPHIS AREA VO-TECH SCHOOL, Memphis, Tennessee, 1986-1988
Instructor/Coordinator, EMT/Paramedic Programs

♦ Established and managed all aspects of paramedic training program. Built relationships; negotiated and secured contracts with regional medical center and local emergency medical services.

GREEN AMBULANCE SERVICE, Memphis, Tennessee, 1984-1987
Paramedic Supervisor

♦ Supervised daily operations and coordinated continuing education for emergency medical staff. Acted as liaison with hospital and medical staff.

FIRE & EMS DEPARTMENT, Nashville, Tennessee, 1978-1984
EMT, Firefighter/Engineer

♦ Acquired expertise in fire suppression, equipment operations, and rescue techniques. Provided ALS patient care as member of an ALS medical crew.

EDUCATION

Certificate, Human Resources Management, Tulane University, New Orleans, Louisiana, 1995

Master of Science, Emergency Health Services Administration, Thesis pending, Louisiana State University Medical Center, New Orleans, Louisiana, anticipated completion November 1997

Bachelor of Arts, School of Business and Management, Tulane University, New Orleans, Louisiana, 1993

CERTIFICATIONS

NREMT-Paramedic	State of Louisiana Paramedic
ACLS Instructor, Louisiana & New Orleans Affiliate	ACLS Course Co-Director, Louisiana
BLS Instructor/Trainer, A.H.A. Louisiana Affiliate	BLS Instructor, Louisiana
PALS Provider	

PROFESSIONAL AFFILIATIONS

Member, Board of Directors, New Orleans EMS Council, Louisiana
Affiliate Faculty, ACLS, American Heart Association, Louisiana Affiliate
Volunteer Paramedic, Bourbon Street Rescue Squad
Regional ALS Trainer, New Orleans EMS Council, Louisiana

ALEXANDER D. HAMMER

65-33 Main Coast, Eastbourne, East Sussex, England BN21 4EQ

0323 XXXXX (Fax) 0323 XXXXX

CAREER SUMMARY

Energetic senior executive with solid achievements in the hospitality industry. A resourceful and innovative leader willing to take risks, pursue new ideas, experiences, and techniques while meeting or exceeding aggressive financial goals.

Adept at analyzing complex business issues and producing "common sense" solutions. Demonstrated ability to develop and maintain team atmosphere. Hands-on experience in leading a culturally diverse workforce.

EXPERIENCE

GRAND INTERNATIONAL INC., 1974-present

GENERAL MANAGER, Park Hotel, Eastbourne, England, 1995-present

Selected to lead the acquisition and refurbishment of this 85 year-old landmark hotel, Grand's first in England.

- In 1996, improved total hotel sales by 9% and total house profit by 21% over 1995 levels. Significantly improved guest and associate satisfaction results.
- Designed and implemented plans to permanently reduce staffing levels from 344 in 1995 to 295 by year-end 1996.
- Completed $10 million total hotel refurbishment within budget and on schedule.
- Guided development and implementation of hotel's first ever merit pay, succession planning, and comprehensive training programs for management and hourly associates.
- Established Grand name through involvement with the U.S. Embassy and various British hotel schools.

GENERAL MANAGER, Chicago Grand Hotel, Chicago, Illinois, 1989-1995

Total management responsibility for a full-service 410-room metropolitan hotel.

- Exceeded total hotel sales, profit, and associate satisfaction goals in 1994. Improved guest satisfaction in 1994 by 105% over 1993 results.
- Improved House Profit margin from 27.7% in 1990 to 32% in 1994.
- Innovator behind the conversion of Scrabble's Lounge to the Starlight's Night Club concept, resulting in annual sales increasing from $300,000 to $2.2 million. As a result, received "President's Special Achievement Award" in 1992.
- Consistently completed all capital improvement projects on time and within budget, including total rooms re-do in 1992 and complete ballroom and lobby refurbishment in 1993.
- Designed a leaner, more efficient management structure, reducing staff from 36 to 24 and saving $675,000 annually in salary and benefits expense.
- Converted full-service associate cafeteria to vending operation, saving $160,000 annually, leading the way for other hotels to adopt this approach.
- Among the first hotels in the region to introduce Viva convenience foods, Peer Review (an improved dispute resolution process for associates), Pre-employment Drug Screening, Pizza King pizza in all food outlets, and Check-list (a check-in improvement process).
- Recognized by owner as "A pro-active hotelier who took a creative approach to managing the hotel in a very dynamic market...a performer with quantifiable results."

ALEXANDER D. HAMMER   PAGE 2

VICE PRESIDENT/SENIOR VICE PRESIDENT HUMAN RESOURCES, Grand Hotels, Resorts, and Suites Division, Chicago, Illinois, 1984-1989

Served as top Human Resources Executive for corporation's largest operating division.

- ◆ Implemented the first comprehensive executive development and succession planning process.

- ◆ Directed successful efforts to establish and maintain non-union status at New York Grand and San Diego Grand.

DIRECTOR, CORPORATE HUMAN RESOURCES PLANNING/DEVELOPMENT, Grand Corporate Human Resources Department, Chicago, Illinois, 1983-1984

Led human resources activities during acquisition of Grand's first lodging venture in Paris, France.

- ◆ Guided management efforts during successful de-unionization drive.

DIRECTOR, EMPLOYEE RELATIONS, Grand Corporate Human Resources Department, Chicago, Illinois, 1980-1983

Supervised the administration of company-wide Employee Opinion Survey Program.

MANAGER, PERSONNEL SERVICES, Grand Corporation, Chicago, Illinois, 1979-1980

Performed generalist human resources activities with primary focus on maintaining non-union status.

CORPORATE-LEVEL HUMAN RESOURCES POSITIONS, Grand Corporate Human Resources Department, Chicago, Illinois, 1974-1979

Progressive experience including Compensation Analyst, Employee Relations Representative, Benefits Analyst, and Equal Employment Opportunity Representative.

EDUCATION

B.A., Government and Politics, Chicago State University, Chicago, Illinois, 1974

Completed the **New York University Advanced Professional Development Program for Human Resource Executives**, July 1984

SKILLS

Conversant in French

ALISSON T. WILSON
763 Sunset Plaza, Phoenix, Arizona 85002
(602) XXX-XXXX

REGISTERED OPTICIAN

Extensive experience with dispensing, lab work, contact lens, refractive knowledge, and satisfying patient needs. Work effectively with representatives of frames and lens companies.

CAREER HIGHLIGHTS

- Established Sunset Ridge Optical. Designed and oversaw building construction; staffed office and managed operation.

- Planned and managed total renovation and revitalization of Sun City Optical, Phoenix, Arizona. Scheduled appointments, provided patient care, and dispensed all eye wear. Handled all accounts receivable and accounts payable.

- Designed, set up and operated office for ophthalmologist. Administered patient care and dispensed eyeglasses, contact lens, and prosthetic devices. Hired and trained new optician.

- Expertise in establishing and building optical practices. Effectively devise strategies to compete in the marketplace.

- Proven record in managing optical practices to maximize profitability.

- Skilled in providing quality patient care and diplomatically resolving patient needs/problems.

WORK HISTORY

Registered Optician, Sun City Optical, Sun City, Arizona, 1994-1995
Registered Optician, Sunset Ridge Optical, Phoenix, Arizona, 1987-1994
Registered Optician, Scottsdale Optical, Scottsdale, Arizona, 1982-1992
Registered Optician, Alisson T. Wilson, Phoenix, Arizona, 1963-1982

EDUCATION

B.A. in Business Administration, Drake University, Des Moines, Iowa, 1962

LICENSES/CERTIFICATIONS

Registered Optician Arizona, 1963
Parabolar Contact Lens Certificate, Peters & Smith, Inc., Sacramento, California, 1963
Prosthetic Eye Study at Jardon Plastics Research, Inc., Detroit, Michigan, 1966
Arizona State Board of Certified Opticians, 1973
Arizona State Board of Contact Lens Fitting, 1983

NANCY MARTINS

8 Woodlawn Drive
Long Island City, New York 11100
(718) XXX-XXXX

QUALIFICATIONS SUMMARY

Highly skilled and resourceful New York City police investigator with a strong interest in protecting children. Extensive experience in investigating and solving serious crimes involving children. Reputation for excellence and providing high quality service to city and outside agencies.

POLICE EXPERIENCE

NEW YORK CITY POLICE DEPARTMENT, 1972-present

Crime Scene Investigator, Crime Scene Section, 1981-present

- Respond to major crime scenes to locate and document physical evidence through visual examination, photography, and collection.
- Examine physical evidence collected by other officers for latent prints. The resulting evidence is protected and prepared for presentation in a court of law. Directly involved in keeping the section current on the latest trends in crime scene approach and the development of latent prints.

Investigation

- Extensive experience investigating crimes, collecting data, and interrogating witnesses and potential suspects.
- Follow established procedures in investigating and collecting potential evidence.
- In-depth training and hands-on experience in evaluating and determining injuries.
- Testified and appeared as an expert witness in numerous court proceedings.

Documentation

- Thorough and extensive experience documenting serious crimes.
- Accurate and precise report writing skills resulting in acceptance of all reports in a court of law.
- Certified as an expert in documentation of evidence in State and Federal courts.

Patrol Officer, Patrol Division, 1973-1981

- Performed all tasks associated with first responder police services, general patrol duties, field training officer, and accident investigation unit.
- Made appropriate decisions to either extend a warning or initiate severe action.

Police Cadet, 1972-1973

- Completed various administrative assignments within the Police Department.

NANCY MARTINS   PAGE 2

TRAINING EXPERIENCE

Instructor, 1986-1992
New York City Police Academy

Directly supervised the Advanced Crime Scene Procedure mandatory in-service retraining course.

Lecturer, 1983-present
New York City Department of Human Services
City Health Systems, Sexual Assault Nurses
Suffolk County Community College
John Jay Forensic Science Academy
New York City Criminal Justice Academy
New York City Public Safety Academy

Create curriculum and conduct classes on crime scene investigations.

SKILLS

Photography, latent print development, crime scene reconstruction, New York State Certified Instructor for Crime Scene Documentation.

PROFESSIONAL TRAINING

New York City Police Academy: Deviant Groups, 1994, Interview and Interrogation, 1992
FBI Academy: Latent & Advanced Fingerprint Photography and Training, 1982, 1986, 1991
John Jay Forensic Science Academy, 1983, 1986, 1989
Police Institute, Pace College: Homicide Investigation School, 1988
Suffolk County Community College, 1986, 1988
New York City Criminal Justice Academy, 1972, 1981, 1982
Kodak Photography School, 1981

HONORS/AWARDS

New York City, **Policeman of the Year**, 1992
New York City, **Outstanding Performance Award**, 1992
New York City, **Meritorious Award**, 1985

PROFESSIONAL AFFILIATIONS

International Association for Identification: Certified Senior Crime Scene Analyst, 1990
John Jay Forensic Science Alumni Association: President, 1990-1992, Board of Directors, 1983-1990

ROBERT L. DRYDEN

8712 Palm Drive
Culver City, California 90224
Work (310) XXX-XXX Home (310) XXX-XXXX

PROFESSIONAL PROFILE

Experienced programmer analyst with expertise in COBOL, JCL, MVS, VSAM, CICS, and DB2 software applications.

♦ Progressive background in software design/development, structured analysis and design techniques, software development life cycle, software development methodology, information engineering, CASE tools, process modeling, data modeling, quality assurance, and software evaluation.

♦ Trained in Visual Basic, experienced with client server applications, and strong interest in working with two and three tier application systems.

COMPUTER SKILLS

COBOL II, FoxBase, SqlBase by Gupta, DB2, CICS, Lotus Notes, TSO/SPF, Clist, OS/MVS/XA, Image/View, Assembler, Novell Netware, Application Development System (ADS), Lotus 1-2-3, Easy Flow, WordPerfect.

EXPERIENCE

PROGRAMMER/ANALYST
Pacific Coast Credit Union, Los Angeles, California, 1993 - present

♦ Participate in a business re-engineering effort utilizing CASE tools and Yourdon methodology; gather requirements using JAD sessions.

♦ Write functional specifications for Mortgage and a Member Record image/work flow systems including reports, definition of queues, file updates, definition of maturation dates for documents on DASD, optical, and shelf life, and new screen developments. Define document forms, tabs, folder layouts, and collection types.

♦ Communicate effectively with department heads and key staff members to identify individual department needs/requirements. Program system to generate reports to satisfy needs.

♦ Implemented and customized a purchased subsystem, VSR, which inserted electronic coded documents into the Image Plus database. Gathered requirements for new reports; maintained and enhanced the systems. Utilized JCL, COBOL II, CICS, and DB2 in programming efforts.

♦ Conceived and implemented method to produce customized access to organize reporting requirements by department.

PROGRAMMER/ANALYST
Technical Support Services, Los Angeles, California, 1990 - 1993

♦ Enhanced and maintained a COBOL- and VSAM-based payroll system. Prepared files, created reports, and modified existing code as requested by oil company officials. This system processed worldwide employees wages for Union Oil Company.

ROBERT L. DRYDEN PAGE 2

LEADER/SENIOR SYSTEMS ANALYST
Federal Support Inc.(FSI), Washington, D.C., 1988 - 1990

♦ Supported a contract for Federal Emergency Management Agency (FEMA). Installed, maintained, developed, and trained in support of a FoxBase audit system, HelpLAN. Gathered client requirements and wrote detail specifications. The system tracked the accomplishments of the U.S. Corp of Engineers along with the expenditures incurred for the disaster superfund.

♦ Served as site leader for two offices within the General Service Administration (GSA). Scheduled production, maintained and developed the existing systems, established a new system using a client server DBMS (SQLBase), and downsized a COBOL system into a SQLBase system. Assigned work to team members, provided quality assurance, scheduled and tracked all assignments, produced status and financial reports, recommended new hires, and directed communications between GSA and FSI staffs.

♦ Successfully delivered diverse projects on time. Wrote benchmark and prototype specifications, evaluated and recommended a client server DBMS; developed and implemented an audit sub-system; wrote general and detail design documents.

PROGRAMMER ANALYST
The Computer Company, Los Angeles, California, 1986 - 1988

♦ Developed a reutilization system on Convergent Technology hardware (alias the C-3 NGEN) employing an ADS data base for the Pentagon's excess automatic data processing equipment, EEIS. The reutilization system was successfully implemented and now operates in an on-line production environment. The EEIS developmental project was completed.

♦ Headed a project to re-design the ADPE data system onto client server platform.

PROGRAMMER ANALYST
Sun Insurance Company, San Diego, California, 1983 - 1985

♦ Maintained and enhanced an Accounting, Budget and Cost (ABC) system, a major financial system containing approximately 60 different jobs.

♦ Aided development of a sub system, referred to as the Cost Allocation System (CAS), developed in order to produce Profit and Loss Statements and other accounting reports.

EDUCATION

San Diego Mesa College, San Diego, California
    Master level courses in Information Systems

University of California, Los Angeles, Los Angeles, California
    Certificate, Post Graduate Studies in Information Systems, 1982
    Bachelor of Science, Administrative and Management,1980

ROBERT L. DRYDEN

8712 Palm Drive
Culver City, California 90224
Work (310) XXX-XXX Home (310) XXX-XXXX

SUMMARY

Experienced programmer analyst with expertise in COBOL, JCL, MVS, VSAM, CICS, and DB2 software applications.

Progressive background in software design/development, structured analysis and design techniques, software development life cycle, software development methodology, information engineering, CASE tools, process modeling, data modeling, quality assurance, and software evaluation.

Trained in Visual Basic, experienced with client server applications, and strong interest in working with two and three tier application systems.

COMPUTER SKILLS

COBOL II, FoxBase, SqlBase by Gupta, DB2, CICS, Lotus Notes, TSO/SPF, Clist, OS/MVS/XA, Image/View, Assembler, Novell Netware, Application Development System (ADS), Lotus 1-2-3, Easy Flow, WordPerfect.

EXPERIENCE

PROGRAMMER/ANALYST
   Pacific Coast Credit Union, Los Angeles, California, 1993 - present

Participate in a business re-engineering effort utilizing CASE tools and Yourdon methodology; gather requirements using JAD sessions.

Write functional specifications for Mortgage and a Member Record image/work flow systems including reports, definition of queues, file updates, definition of maturation dates for documents on DASD, optical, and shelf life, and new screen developments. Define document forms, tabs, folder layouts, and collection types.

Communicate effectively with department heads and key staff members to identify individual department needs/requirements. Program system to generate reports to satisfy needs.

Implemented and customized a purchased subsystem, VSR, which inserted electronic coded documents into the Image Plus database. Gathered additional requirements for new reports; maintained and enhanced the current systems. Utilized JCL, COBOL II, CICS, and DB2 in programming efforts.

Conceived and implemented method to produce customized access to organize reporting requirements by department.

PROGRAMMER/ANALYST
   Technical Support Services, Los Angeles, California, 1990 - 1993

Enhanced and maintained a COBOL- and VSAM-based payroll system. Prepared files, created reports, and modified existing code as requested by oil company officials. This system processed worldwide employees wages for Union Oil Company.

ROBERT L. DRYDEN   PAGE 2

LEADER/SENIOR SYSTEMS ANALYST
Federal Support Inc.(FSI), Washington, D.C., 1988 - 1990

Supported a contract for Federal Emergency Management Agency (FEMA). Installed, maintained, developed, and trained in support of a FoxBase audit system, HelpLAN. Gathered client requirements and wrote detail specifications. The system tracked the accomplishments of the U.S. Corp of Engineers along with the expenditures incurred for the disaster superfund.

Served as site leader for two offices within the General Service Administration (GSA). Scheduled production, maintained and developed the existing systems, established a new system using a client server DBMS (SQLBase), and downsized a COBOL system into a SQLBase system. Assigned work to team members, provided quality assurance, scheduled and tracked all assignments, produced status and financial reports, recommended new hires, and directed communications between GSA and FSI staffs.

Successfully delivered diverse projects on time. Wrote benchmark and prototype specifications, evaluated and recommended a client server DBMS; developed and implemented an audit sub-system; wrote general and detail design documents.

PROGRAMMER ANALYST
The Computer Company, Los Angeles, California, 1986 - 1988

Developed a reutilization system on Convergent Technology hardware (alias the C-3 NGEN) employing an ADS data base for the Pentagon's excess automatic data processing equipment, EEIS. The reutilization system was successfully implemented and now operates in an on-line production environment. The EEIS developmental project was completed.

Headed a project to re-design the ADPE data system onto client server platform.

PROGRAMMER ANALYST
Sun Insurance Company, San Diego, California, 1983 - 1985

Maintained and enhanced an Accounting, Budget and Cost (ABC) system, a major financial system containing approximately 60 different jobs.

Aided development of a sub system, referred to as the Cost Allocation System (CAS), developed in order to produce Profit and Loss Statements and other accounting reports.

EDUCATION

San Diego Mesa College, San Diego, California
Master level courses in Information Systems

University of California, Los Angeles, Los Angeles, California
Certificate, Post Graduate Studies in Information Systems, 1982
Bachelor of Science, Administrative and Management,1980

ROBERT L. DRYDEN
8712 Palm Drive
Culver City, California 90224
Work (310) XXX-XXXX
Home (310) XXX-XXXX

SUMMARY

Experienced programmer analyst with expertise in COBOL, JCL, MVS, VSAM, CICS, and DB2 software applications.

Progressive background in software design/development, structured analysis and design techniques, software development life cycle, software development methodology, information engineering, CASE tools, process modeling, data modeling, quality assurance, and software evaluation.

Trained in Visual Basic, experienced with client server applications, and strong interest in working with two and three tier application systems.

COMPUTER SKILLS

COBOL II, FoxBase, SqlBase by Gupta, DB2, CICS, Lotus Notes, TSO/SPF, Clist, OS/MVS/XA, Image/View, Assembler, Novell Netware, Application Development System (ADS), Lotus 1-2-3, Easy Flow, WordPerfect.

EXPERIENCE

PROGRAMMER/ANALYST
Pacific Coast Credit Union, Los Angeles, California, 1993 - present

Participate in a business re-engineering effort utilizing CASE tools and Yourdon methodology; gather requirements using JAD sessions.

Write functional specifications for Mortgage and a Member Record image/work flow systems including reports, definition of queues, file updates, definition of maturation dates for documents on DASD, optical, and shelf life, and new screen developments. Define document forms, tabs, folder layouts, and collection types.

Communicate effectively with department heads and key staff members to identify individual department needs/requirements. Program system to generate reports to satisfy needs.

Implemented and customized a purchased subsystem, VSR, which inserted electronic coded documents into the Image Plus database. Gathered additional requirements for new reports; maintained and enhanced the current systems. Utilized JCL, COBOL II, CICS, and DB2 in programming efforts.

Conceived and implemented method to produce customized access to organize reporting requirements by department.

PROGRAMMER/ANALYST
Technical Support Services, Los Angeles, California, 1990 - 1992

Enhanced and maintained a COBOL- and VSAM-based payroll system. Prepared files, created reports, and modified existing code as requested by oil company officials. This system processed worldwide employees wages for Union Oil Company.

LEADER/SENIOR SYSTEMS ANALYST
Federal Support Inc.(FSI), Washington, D.C., 1988 - 1990

Supported a contract for Federal Emergency Management Agency (FEMA). Installed, maintained, developed, and trained in support of a FoxBase audit system, HelpLAN. Gathered client requirements and wrote detail specifications. The system tracked the accomplishments of the U.S. Corp of Engineers along with the expenditures incurred for the disaster superfund.

Served as site leader for two offices within the General Service Administration (GSA). Scheduled production, maintained and developed the existing systems, established a new system using a client server DBMS (SQLBase), and downsized a COBOL system into a SQLBase system. Assigned work to team members, provided quality assurance, scheduled and tracked all assignments, produced status and financial reports, recommended new hires, and directed communications between GSA and FSI staffs.

Successfully delivered diverse projects on time. Wrote benchmark and prototype specifications, evaluated and recommended a client server DBMS; developed and implemented an audit sub-system; wrote general and detail design documents.

PROGRAMMER ANALYST
The Computer Company, Los Angeles, California, 1986 - 1988

Developed a reutilization system on Convergent Technology hardware (alias the C-3 NGEN) employing an ADS data base for the Pentagon's excess automatic data processing equipment, EEIS. The reutilization system was successfully implemented and now operates in an on-line production environment. The EEIS developmental project was completed.

Headed a project to re-design the ADPE data system onto client server platform.

PROGRAMMER ANALYST
Sun Insurance Company, San Diego, California, 1983 - 1985

Maintained and enhanced an Accounting, Budget and Cost (ABC) system, a major financial system containing approximately 60 different jobs. Aided development of a sub system, referred to as the Cost Allocation System (CAS), developed in order to produce Profit and Loss Statements and other accounting reports.

EDUCATION

San Diego Mesa College, San Diego, California
Master level courses in Information Systems

University of California, Los Angeles, Los Angeles, California
Certificate, Post Graduate Studies in Information Systems, 1982
Bachelor of Science, Administrative and Management, 1980

THERESA O'BRIEN
98 Pecan Street
Houston, Texas 77060
(713) XXX-XXXX

QUALIFICATIONS SUMMARY

Enthusiastic and dedicated clinician with a specialty in trauma, children of divorce, relationships and intimacy, and career development. Expertise in coaching and motivating clients in self discovery and active problem solving.

PROFESSIONAL EXPERIENCE

Clinical Assessment and Psychotherapy

- Provide adults, families, adolescents, and children with extensive psychotherapy services for depression, anxiety and panic attacks, surviving trauma or abuse, sexuality issues, children of divorce and blended families, stress and chronic illness, addiction relapse prevention, relationships and intimacy, shame and self-esteem, anger and conflict resolution, loss and grief, and career development.

- Assess clients and develop treatment plans for individuals, couples, and groups including brief therapy, crisis intervention, and long-term treatment.

- Apply and combine hypnotherapy and meditation approaches with psychoanalytic techniques to foster change.

- Prepare treatment summaries and documents required for case evaluation and third party reimbursement. Evaluate treatment outcomes; implement termination, referral, and follow-up activities.

Consulting

- Supervise mental health professionals obtaining credentials, building private practices, and developing client treatment plans.

- Cultivate effective relationships and linkages with community agencies, organizations, and other professionals.

- Develop innovative approaches for practitioners, groups, and organizations that promote client change, conflict resolution, and collaborative effort.

Training and Development

- Create psychoeducational programs and teach adolescents and adults to actively problem solve, develop coping skills, and understand physical and emotional healing processes.

- Implement, administer, evaluate, and revise programs for the delivery of counseling and related services.

- Customize and deliver team building and wellness programs for diverse audiences.

EDUCATION

M.Ed., Community Mental Health Counseling, 1988
Texas A&M University, College Station, Texas

B.A., Psychology, 1982
Texas Southern University, Houston, Texas

THERESA O'BRIEN   PAGE 2

EMPLOYMENT HISTORY

Houston County, Houston, Texas
   Management Analyst (Strategic Planner), 1989-present

   Management Analyst (Educator, Group Facilitator), 1988-1989

Private Psychotherapy Practice, Houston, Texas
   Licensed Professional Counselor, 1992-present

Dr. Peter Jones, Professional Counseling Services, Private Practice, Galveston, Texas
   Mental Health Caseworker, 1990-1992

Women's Center of Beaumont, Beaumont, Texas
   Mental Health Counselor, 1989-1990

Health and Human Services, Family Support Administration, Austin, Texas
   Program and Management Analyst, 1982-1988

HOUSTON COUNTY AWARDS AND HONORS

Outstanding Performance Award: Program development services, Department of Animal Control, 1994; Business Process Redesign Project, Department of Purchasing and Supply Management, 1994 and Office of Personnel, 1994
Letter of Commendation: Department of Animal Control, 1993
Certificate of Recognition: Houston County Training Consortium, 1992
Certificate of Award: Office for Children, 1991-1992

LICENSES AND CERTIFICATIONS

Certified Hypnotherapist, Eastern Institute of Hypnotherapy, 1994
Licensed Professional Counselor, State of Texas, 1992
Licensed Mental Health Counselor, State of Texas, 1992
National Board Certified Counselor, National Board of Certified Counselors, 1991

PROFESSIONAL TRAINING

Eastern Institute of Hypnotherapy
   Hypnotherapy Certification Program, 1994
Texas Southern University
   Strategies for Working with Dysfunctional Families, 1992; Improving Instruction Through Group Dynamics, 1991; Human Development, 1991; Multi-cultural Counseling, 1991
Texas A&M
   Current Topics in Adolescent Counseling, 1992; Healing the Incest Wound, 1992; Child Sexual Abuse, 1992; Counseling Persons with HIV and AIDS, 1992
Lamar University
   Sexual Issues and the Helping Professional, 1991; Counseling Lesbian and Gays, 1991
University of Texas Health Science Center at Houston
   Psychopathology, 1993

PROFESSIONAL AFFILIATIONS

American Counselors Association, Texas Counselors Association, American Mental Health Counselors Association

SUSANNA WORTH
7881 Willow Drive, Winston-Salem, North Carolina 27100
(919) XXX-XXXX

CAREER OBJECTIVE

Dedicated, hard working, and organized individual with a solid background in the biological sciences, seeks an opportunity to build a career in the field of health care.

EDUCATION

Bachelor of Science in Biology, Columbia College, Columbia, South Carolina, 1996

Certifications in adult CPR, choking, first aid; pursuing the AFAA Primary Certification Review

40 credits in the biological sciences:

- General Biology
- Parasitology
- Physical Chemistry
- Microbiology
- Nutrition
- Genetics
- Evolution
- Cellular Biology
- Invertebrate Zoology
- General Chemistry
- Entomology
- Plant Ecology

RELATED EXPERIENCE

Laboratory Assistant, Columbia College, Columbia, South Carolina, Spring 1996, Fall 1995

Measured, mixed, and prepared chemicals for separation of chlorophyll extraction and DNA gel electrophoresis.

Researcher, Columbia College, Columbia, South Carolina, Spring 1996

Conducted senior research project and experiment to test the physiological functions of taste buds. Developed research skills, prepared scientific report, and presented findings to science students and faculty members.

Aerobics Instructor, Columbia Recreation Department, Columbia, South Carolina, 1994-1996

Instructed aerobics classes; choreographed routines to meet multi-level abilities of participants. Ensured individual safety of participants; monitored heart rates and proper body alignment.

EXPERIENCE

Nutrition Assistant, Weight Loss Inc., Winston-Salem, North Carolina, Summer 1996

Provided responsive care to clients regarding weight loss. Assessed client health history and selected an appropriate individual meal plan. Instructed clients regarding nutrition, meal planning, and increased physical activity; maintained weekly client progress reports. Encouraged clients to identify and resolve weight loss impediments and concerns while maintaining client confidentiality.

Sales Assistant, Nutritionally Yours, Winston-Salem, North Carolina, Summer 1995

Assisted customers in selection and cash and credit sales transactions for a national retail operation specializing in natural grocery products.

HONORS AND AWARDS

Columbia College Scholarship, four years; **Milton Scholarship,** four years; **National Science Foundation Scholarship,** two years.

SKILLS

Proficient with IBM PC, WordPerfect, Microsoft Word, and Excel.

STEPHEN NORTH
9700 Sixth Avenue
Louisville, Kentucky 40220
Work (502) XXX-XXXX   Home (502) XXX-XXXX

QUALIFICATIONS SUMMARY

Results-oriented sales professional with superior selling skills. Natural sales ability with an aggressive and persistent approach to identifying and closing sales.

EXPERIENCE

Senior Account Executive, 1993-present
USA Telecommunications Inc., Louisville, Kentucky

Successfully sell state-of-the-art telecommunications products in a four-state territory. Consistently increase sales by creating distribution channels, establishing major accounts, cultivating new business, and retaining existing accounts.

SELECTED ACCOMPLISHMENTS

- Currently 134% over quota for 1997.

- The top national sales producer, 1996.

- Doubled territory sales in the initial nine months by effectively planning account strategies while identifying and satisfying customer needs.

- Tripled individual annual sales from $1.2 million in 1994 to over $3 million in 1996.

- Closed the largest individual contract - a $700,000 sale to the Commonwealth of Kentucky.

- Selected "Top Account Executive" for 3rd and 4th Quarter, 1996.

- Produced 125% over quota for 1995, performing #2 nationwide.

- Sold over $1.2 million in 1994, ranking #4 out of 70 nationwide account executives.

- Awarded "President's Club" in 1994, 1995, 1996.

Marketing Representative, 1992-1993
Business Systems, Lexington, Kentucky

Sold computer systems to independent retailers in the Commonwealth of Kentucky. Completed rigorous six-month training program, finishing first in class.

Expanded client base and cultivated new business through canvassing, cold calls, detailed product demonstrations, and effective proposals.

EDUCATION

Bachelor of Business Administration, major Marketing, 1992
Centre College, Danville, Kentucky

FRANK MARCIANO
2 Main Street, Philadelphia, Pennsylvania 19132   (215) XXX-XXXX

PROFESSIONAL PROFILE

Successful sales manager with extensive experience building and managing sales operations and developing sales staff and markets to consistently exceed goals.

EXPERIENCE

LIBERTY MUSIC COMPANY, 1986-present
STORE MANAGER, Philadelphia, Pennsylvania, 1995-present

- Manage operations and staff of piano showroom with annual sales of $2.6 to $3 million. Hire, train, schedule staff; evaluate performance.

- Establish, monitor, and consistently achieve/exceed sales goals.

- Implement strategies that successfully penetrate new markets and expand business.

- Increased sales 20% in first year by developing effective merchandising techniques including student education programs and recital activities.

- Recognized as one of the top ten sales performers since 1986.

GENERAL MANAGER, Pittsburgh, Pennsylvania, 1992-1995

- Directed operations at 2 piano and organ retail establishments. Grew annual sales from $1.7 million to over $2.5 million.

- Oversaw institutional and retail sales, delivery, and service. Managed a staff of 20.

- Grew and developed education program, increasing participation and revenues.

- Initiated outside sales events, maximizing product exposure and generating new business.

SALES MANAGER, Philadelphia, Pennsylvania, 1986-1992

- Promoted to manage flagship piano and organ store at Harper Mills Mall, with annual sales of $2 million.

- Supervised eight employees. Directed in-store promotions, educational sales, outside marketing events, and trade show participation.

FRANK MARCIANO   PAGE 2

ASHBURN PIANO AND ORGAN COMPANY, 1978-1986
MANAGER, Reading, Pennsylvania, 1982-1986

- Promoted to manage Flint Hill Mall store operations with full profit and loss responsibilities for the profit center. Continually improved annual sales volume and profits.

- Recruited, trained, motivated, and evaluated 12 sales and teaching staff members.

- Prepared strategic marketing plans, sales forecasts, and operating budgets. Devised and conducted store and product promotions; handled all advertising and customer relations. Selected merchandise and controlled inventory. Oversaw cost analysis, control, and bookkeeping operations.

- Ranked among top five sales associates in the company.

MANAGER, Harrisburg, Pennsylvania, 1978-1982

- Progressed from sales associate to store manager at Pine Valley Mall.

- Managed store operations, transforming store performance from a loss to the most profitable one in the 25-store chain.

ALLENTOWN SCHOOL DISTRICT, 1976-1978
MUSIC INSTRUCTOR, Allentown, Pennsylvania, 1976-1978

- Directed elementary school music program. Taught students and gave private instruction.

EDUCATION

Bachelor of Science in Music Education, 1976
Saint Joseph's University, Philadelphia, Pennsylvania

Bachelor of Arts in Liberal Studies with a cognate in Music, 1974
Temple University, Philadelphia, Pennsylvania

Professional Development
Completed sales training programs with Tom Hopkins, Karrass Associates, NAMM Management Seminars and at manufacturing facilities of Steinway, Young Chang, and Kimball

RITA A. SHELTON
77 Hill Street, St. Louis, Missouri 63111
Work (314) XXX-XXXX E-mail Abcdef@aol.com

PROFESSIONAL PROFILE

Trained LAN Administrator with certification as a Microsoft® Certified Systems Engineer (MCSE). Solid background installing, configuring, and troubleshooting Microsoft® Windows network systems with emphasis on Microsoft® Windows NT 3.51 and Microsoft® Windows® 95.

Over 11 years of experience with complete installation, configuration, and troubleshooting of 386-, 486-, and Pentium-based computer, CD-ROM, Video Adapter Board, modem, and soundboard installations.

EDUCATION

Microsoft® Certified Systems Engineer (MCSE), Computer Learning International, St. Louis, Missouri, 1996

Anticipate **B. S. in Business Administration**, Washington University, St. Louis, Missouri, May 1997

A. S. in Industrial Engineering, Mission College, Santa Clara, California, 1983

EXPERIENCE

Hyper Technologies, Inc., St. Louis, Missouri
***WINDOWS NT* DEVELOPMENT ENGINEER**, July 1996-present

- Team in developing Windows NT-based web hosting site solutions for small- to large-scale organizations. Utilize Microsoft-based products including Internet Information Server, SQL Server, Merchant Server, and Normandy Server.

Computer Learning International, St. Louis, Missouri
STUDENT, April 22, 1996-June 30, 1996

- Acquired expertise to install, configure, troubleshoot, optimize, and support Windows® NT Workstation and Server, Windows® 95, Microsoft® System Management Server (SMS), Microsoft® Windows for Workgroups / Windows® 3.x Configuration, and Microsoft® TCP/IP Internetworking on Windows NT. Gained technical ability to establish network and resource security and integrate Windows® with other technologies such as Novell® Netware.

The Federal Systems Company (formerly ABC Federal Systems), San Francisco, California
FINANCIAL ANALYST, 1994-1996

- Managed financial information for 6 Navy systems contracts worth over $144 million in revenue. Reviewed and prepared monthly financial and analytical reports including revenues, profit determination, and workload reporting/tracking. Analyzed and resolved budget variances.

- Provided formal quarterly estimate-at-completion reports for each contract. Supported contracts monthly requiring Contract Performance Report and Cost/Schedule Status Report.

- Developed budgetary changes as funding levels increased and rebaselined the contracts as negotiations were completed. Conducted business/financial condition reviews with senior management to ensure technical/financial success. Prepared the yearly budgets for on-going contracts. Assisted in cost proposals for new business development. Responded to all audit requests from the Defense Contracts Audit Agency (DCAA) concerning Navy contract expenditures.

RITA A. SHELTON   PAGE 2

ABC Federal Systems, San Francisco, California, 1982-1994
LEAD COST ACCOUNTANT, 1992-1994, **COST ACCOUNTANT**, 1989-1992

- Handled the hardware cost tracking and allocation to Navy contracts totaling $80 million in work-in-process (WIP) cost. Performed labor audits to ensure accurate labor-booking for all WIP orders.

- Completed physical audit and reporting for stockroom, vendor consigned, and WIP inventories. Served on the inventory reconciliation task force.

- Recovered $18 million of otherwise non-billable costs by utilizing knowledge of the perpetual inventory system; identified and linked WIP non-billable stock parts to appropriate Navy contracts.

- Identified, mitigated, and implemented changes to highlight $17 million of unidentified IBM inventory residing at subcontractor's location.

- Administered the first automated reporting system, replacing the manual reporting of stockroom, WIP, and vendor consigned inventory audits.

PRODUCTION CONTROL ANALYST, 1982-1989

- Worked with a variety of ground- and sea-launched cruise missile systems. Tracked and reported production hardware. Constructed and maintained configuration plans for hardware schedule deliveries that met delivery requirements. Prevented deviations to schedule by expediting potentially late items. Maintained the cost integrity of in-process hardware units and the prevention of excess inventory.

- Completed delivery of the last hardware unit six months ahead of schedule. Took on the additional task of Production Control Coordinator, a vacant position for nine months.

- Recognized by management for the prevention of current and future impacts to schedule, excellent follow-up techniques on problem prevention, and timely escalation of issues needing management involvement. Cited for role in implementing plans to meet on-time schedule requirements.

SOFTWARE EXPERIENCE

- Excel
- WordPerfect
- Windows® 95
- Microsoft® Systems Management Server

- Word
- PowerPoint
- Windows® NT Workstation and Server
- Merchant Server

- Freelance
- Quattro Pro

- Lotus 1-2-3
- Harvard Graphics
- Normandy Server

HARDWARE EXPERIENCE

- Intel 386-, 486-, Pentium-based motherboard installation and troubleshooting
- Hardware component installation, configuration, troubleshooting, and optimization (including video adapter cards, modems, CD-ROM drives, 16-bit soundcards, and diskette drives)

DATABASE EXPERIENCE

- Microsoft®Access
- SAS-TSO

- MDSS (Corporate Ledger System)
- CICS (Generic mainframe database system)

- Lotus Approach
- SQL Server

ABC/THE FEDERAL SYSTEMS COMPANY TRAINING

SEI-CMM Introduction, Government Property Control Management, PCMS (Program Control Management System), Defect Prevention Processes, CPMIC (Contract Performance Management Information Control), Internet Training, Contract Types, Transformational Leadership, TINA (Truth In Negotiations Act), WordPerfect for Windows.

REGINA D. HILL
401 SW 26th Street, Miami, Florida 33170
(305) XXX-XXXX

CAREER SUMMARY

Skilled educator with 23 years of teaching experience. Taught basic concepts in all curricular areas for pre-K through grade 4. Worked with regular and special needs students from a variety of social and economic backgrounds.

EDUCATION

M.Ed., Reading, University of Miami, Coral Gables, Florida, 1983
B.S., Elementary Education, Florida State University, Tallahassee, Florida, 1970

EXPERIENCE

Teacher, St. Mary's Pre-school, Miami, Florida, 1995-present
- Taught three pre-K classes in a diverse environment including bi-lingual and multi-cultural students. Promoted literacy and social development through a play-based program.

Sales Associate, Scholastic Inc., Miami, Florida, 1991-1995
- Conducted presentations and exhibited a wide range of instructional materials for the Northern Miami region of one of the largest educational publication companies. Assisted all school staff in selecting and ordering materials.

Teacher, Ocean Park Pre-school, Coral Gables, Florida, 1991-1995
- Taught a class of 16 four- and five-year olds in a developmental program. Supported and assisted new teachers. Participated in curriculum development. Attended early childhood education workshops and conferences.

Reading Teacher, Bay Elementary School, Miami, Florida, 1988-1989
- Diagnosed and tested high risk, multi-cultural students in reading. Created individualized reading and writing programs to meet student needs. Conducted workshops for parents and participated in evaluating and recommending services for children with learning and emotional problems.

Teacher, Mark Twain Elementary School, Miami, Florida, 1979-1983, 1985-1988
- Taught grades 1-4. Assisted in implementation of the integrated language arts program. Represented staff on Faculty Advisory Council.

Teacher, Sandy Road Elementary School, Coral Gables, Florida, 1978-1979
- Provided structure and direction for second grade class. Worked closely with L.D. and Reading teachers to address special needs.

Teacher, Northside Elementary School, Tallahassee, Florida, 1970-1978
- Taught first grade for seven years; third grade for one. Piloted a Language Experience Approach to Reading Program. Appointed grade level chair.

CERTIFICATION

Florida Post Graduate Professional, K, Elementary 1-7, Reading Specialist. Expired; re-applied and awaiting renewal.

REGINA D. HILL
Social Security # XXX-XX-XXXX
401 SW 26th Street
Miami, Florida 33170
(305) XXX-XXXX

SUMMARY

Skilled educator with 23 years of teaching experience. Taught basic concepts in all curricular areas for pre-K and elementary grades 1 through 4. Work with regular and special needs students from diverse social, multi-cultural, and economic backgrounds.

EDUCATION

M.Ed., Reading, University of Miami, Coral Gables, Florida, 1983

B.S., Elementary Education, Florida State University, Tallahassee, Florida, 1970

ENDORSEMENTS / CERTIFICATIONS

Florida Post Graduate Professional
K, Elementary 1-7, Reading Specialist
Expired; re-applied and currently awaiting renewal

WORK EXPERIENCE

Teacher, St. Mary's Pre-school, Miami, Florida, 1995-present

Taught three pre-K classes in a diverse environment including bi-lingual and multi-cultural students.

Promoted literacy and social development through a play-based program.

Assessed children through anecdotal observations.

Sales Associate, Scholastic Inc., Miami, Florida, 1991-1995

Conducted presentations and exhibited a wide range of instructional materials for the Northern Miami region of one of the largest educational publication companies.

Assisted all school staff in selecting and ordering materials.

Teacher, Ocean Park Pre-school, Coral Gables, Florida, 1991-1995

Taught a class of 16 four- and five-year olds in a developmental program. Lead teacher; supported and assisted new teachers.

Conferred with parents and Child Find to identify children at risk.

Participated in curriculum development. Attended early childhood education workshops and conferences.

Introduced basic computer skills to children.

REGINA D. HILL **PAGE 2**

Reading Teacher, Bay Elementary School, Miami, Florida, 1988-1989

Diagnosed and tested high-risk, multi-cultural students in reading. Created individualized reading and writing programs to meet student needs.

Conducted workshops for parents and participated in evaluating and recommending services for children with learning and emotional problems.

Teacher, Mark Twain Elementary School, Miami, Florida, 1979-1983, 1985-1988

Taught grades 1-4. Assisted in implementation of the integrated language arts program. Utilized computer to develop basic skills.

Grade level chair.

Represented staff on Faculty Advisory Council.

Teacher, Sandy Road Elementary School, Coral Gables, Florida, 1978-1979

Provided structure and direction for second grade class. Worked closely with L.D. and Reading teachers to address special needs.

Teacher, Northside Elementary School, Tallahassee, Florida, 1970-1978

Taught first grade for seven years; third grade for one. Piloted a Language Experience Approach to Reading Program. Appointed grade level chair.

ADDITIONAL TRAINING

Emergent Literacy Course, University of Miami, Coral Gables, Florida, 1995

Seeking endorsement in Early Childhood Special Education
Completed Curriculum and Methods in Early Childhood, Language Development and Disorders, Classroom Management: Theory and Practice

Career Resources

Contact Impact Publications to receive a free annotated listing of career resources or visit their World Wide Web site for a complete listing of hundreds of career resources: *http://www.impactpublications.com.* The following resume and cover letter books are available directly from Impact Publications. Please send you order, along with payment (add $5.00 shipping for first book and $1.50 for each additional one), to:

IMPACT PUBLICATIONS
9104-N Manassas Drive
Manassas Park, VA 20111-2366
Tel. 703/361-7300 or Fax 703/335-9486
E-mail: impactp@impactpublications.com

Orders from individuals must be prepaid by check, moneyorder, Visa, MasterCard, or American Express. We accept telephone, fax, and e-mail orders.

Qty.	TITLES	Price	TOTAL
__	100 Winning Resumes For $100,000+ Jobs	$24.95	_____
__	101 Resumes For Sure-Hire Results	$10.95	_____
__	201 Dynamite Job Search Letters	$19.95	_____
__	201 Winning Cover Letters For $100,000+ Jobs	$24.95	_____
__	Dynamite Cover Letters	$14.95	_____
__	Dynamite Resumes	$14.95	_____
__	Electronic Resumes For the New Job Market	$11.95	_____
__	High Impact Resumes and Letters	$19.95	_____
__	Resume Shortcuts	$14.95	_____
__	Sure-Hire Cover Letters	$10.95	_____
__	Sure-Hire Resumes	$14.95	_____

149

The On-Line Superstore & Warehouse

Hundreds of Terrific Career Resources Conveniently Available On the World Wide Web 24-Hours a Day, 365 Days a Year!

Ever wanted to know what are the newest and best books, directories, newsletters, wall charts, training programs, videos, CD-ROMs, computer software, and kits available to help you land a job, negotiate a higher salary, or start your own business? What about finding a job in Asia or relocating to San Francisco? Are you curious about how to find a job 24-hours a day by using the Internet or what to do after you leave the military? Trying to keep up-to-date on the latest career resources but not able to find the latest catalogs, brochures, or newsletters on today's "best of the best" resources?

Welcome to the first virtual career bookstore on the Internet. Now you're only a "click" away with Impact Publication's electronic solution to the resource challenge. Impact Publications, one of the nation's leading publishers and distributors of career resources, has launched its comprehensive "Career Superstore and Warehouse" on the Internet. The bookstore is jam-packed with the latest resources focusing on several key career areas:

- Alternative jobs and careers
- Self-assessment
- Career planning and job search
- Employers
- Relocation and cities
- Resumes
- Cover letters
- Dress, image, and etiquette
- Education
- Telephone
- Military
- Salaries
- Interviewing
- Nonprofits
- Empowerment
- Self-esteem
- Goal setting
- Executive recruiters
- Entrepreneurship
- Government
- Networking
- Electronic job search
- International jobs
- Travel
- Law
- Training and presentations
- Minorities
- Physically challenged

"This is more than just a bookstore offering lots of product," say Drs. Ron and Caryl Krannich, two of the nation's leading career experts and authors and developers of this on-line bookstore. *"We're an important resource center for libraries, corporations, government, educators, trainers, and career counselors who are constantly defining and redefining this dynamic field. Of the thousands of career resources we review each year, we only select the 'best of the best.'"*

Visit this rich site and you'll quickly discover just about everything you ever wanted to know about finding jobs, changing careers, and starting your own business—including many useful resources that are difficult to find in local bookstores and libraries. The site also includes what's new and hot, tips for success, monthly specials, and a "Military Career Transition Center." Impact's Web address is:

http://www.impactpublications.com